99

Quick
Observations

on

Leadership

By

Craig S. Wagganer

Craig S. Wagganer

To find other books by Craig S.Wagganer, order additional print or electronic copies or to contact the author visit:

www.leadersbridge.com

Cover Design: Craig S. Wagganer

First Edition: August 2015

Published in the USA, KSWuertz Publications

Library of Congress Cataloging- in- Publication Data

Wagganer, Craig S.

99 Quick Observations on Leadership. Craig S. Wagganer 1st Edition

ISBN: 9781516872527

Craig S. Wagganer

Acknowledgements

Leadership is a team effort. No one becomes a leader solely on their own. And leaders lead; that means someone is following. So when an author's name is placed on a book it doesn't tell the whole story.

Many have been involved in the writing of this book. There is my supportive cherished wife, Shirley; and my reassuring children Annie Marie, Zac, and his wife Annie Michelle. My grandchildren (Hannah, Ben and Sarah) also deserve credit. All make me feel like my life is worthwhile and always love me regardless of how I'm feeling. To them this book is dedicated.

Then there is Kim Wuertz; friend first, but also editor and publisher. Without her help this would have been random thoughts printed on a blog that never left the computer.

There are countless others, friends, family, acquaintances without whose contributions to my life would have altered how I see things. In fact, they did alter how I see things and that's the point of my appreciation for them. As you read this if you think you might be one of those people then you probably are.

But first of all there is my Father to whose book I have dedicated my life. I pray His words shape my thoughts and have the greatest influence. From Him I have learned that to lead is to love. A separation of the two is disastrous.

To lead without loving is to embrace power. This is a cheap imitation. To lead with love is to empower others. That is what true leadership is all about.

How This Book Came to Be

This morning I went to make some eggs for breakfast. I decided scrambled. I broke a couple eggs into a bowl, but the third (or maybe it was the fourth) left a little piece of shell in the bowl. My hands were clean, mostly, so I tried to pinch the piece of shell to get it out of the eggs. I couldn't quite catch it. Every time I put my fingers together the little fragment would slip out.

Some of you may know well what I am talking about. Some others of you are primed to give advice, like use one of the egg shell halves to scoop out the broken shell piece. I know better ways to solve the problem than I was using, but it had become a contest. The small fragment of shell, mocking me from its protective bed of egg whites, versus the 250 pound mammoth attacking its place of comfort and rightful place with its egg brothers.

I was not to be deterred. Rather than use a more effective method, I continued to "show it who's boss" and used my fingers to dig for the fragment. Just when I thought I was victorious the tiny sliver broke into two pieces, one in my fingers and the other slipping laughingly away into the egg sanctuary.

It was decision time. How much was I going to let that inanimate object mock me? After all, I was digging through the eggs with my fingers and the eggs were now pretty well scrambled. But that now even tinier sliver of shell was still smiling at me feeling secure from my attempts. I slowed down. My next attempt was more determined and slow. I was able to take finger and thumb, maneuver the sliver to the side of the bowl, and segregate it into captivity.

Somewhere along the line, I went from desiring scrambled eggs to enjoying the chase. It was no longer a thought that I and my wife would be eating the eggs, but could I actually catch this culprit with my bare hands, uh fingers.

Now another decision, do I really want to eat these eggs? My hands were clean, at least I thought so. My wife would also be eating the eggs, would she think my hands were clean enough, or would the whole fiasco turn her against the consumption of the eggs? But then again, only I would know, and the doctor if it came to that. I won't divulge my decision.

Defining leadership is like trying to catch an egg shell fragment in an ocean of eggs. Just about the time you think you have your finger on it, it slips out and the pursuit is back on, again and again. I guess that is why there are so many books written on leadership, so many classes, so many styles, so many answers, and even more questions. There is no one way to define or understand leadership. It is liquid, flowing, moving, redefining, changing, growing, morphing, etc., etc., and so on.

But we all see examples of leadership around us, both good and bad - no need to name names. They influence us and affect us for better, hopefully not for worse. This book is a collection of reflections from what I have observed and continue to observe, and learn, and relearn, etc., etc., and so on.

I do hope you enjoy the musings, and even if it is an accident I hope you learn something. Chase the egg shell, don't worry about catching it. Enjoy the chase. After all, leadership is a journey, not a destination.

Craig S. Wagganer

Introduction

This book is largely a collection of thoughts and impressions. It comes from circumstances I have experienced, movies I have seen, recollections I have had; from just about any source that tricks me into that which I sometimes avoid - thinking.

You may disagree with what you read. In fact, I might, too, when I read it. The idea isn't to give you unblemished instruction, but rather to ignite your thinking and excite your own creativity when it comes to understanding and pursuing leadership.

Here is my desire - read and think. The chapters, if you can call them that, are very short. A couple paragraphs is my usual attention span and then I start to wander off in other directions.

But they are also short so that they don't include too much information for your reaction. The margins are intentionally wide and space is left between chapters so you can jot down your own notes, ideas and observations. I hope that these words would cause you to think and evaluate; and even lead you in some conclusions that are beneficial and helpful to you and others around you.

In the spaces provided take notes. Gather your own ideas. Share them with others. Continue the leadership experience and journey. Maybe sometime we'll have the opportunity to sit down and think out loud together. It would be great to learn from you.

So, let's get started, and please – have fun!

99 Quick Observations on Leadership
Table of Contents

Integrity First	1
Customer Service is Customer Serving	3
Private Leadership is Revealed Publically	5
Passion, Enthusiasm and Leadership	7
Two Different Displays of Leadership	9
Following Directions	13
A New Word for Leadership?	15
Leadership Humor	17
A Leader's Reflection	19
Leadership from the Birds	21
Where Did I Say That?	23
Pride and Joy	25
Unflappable Self-Leadership	29
The Leadership Trickle	31
String Leadership	33
Sales and Self Leadership	35
"CTV" Leadership	39
Bee Leadership	41
Leadership Participation	43
Push or Pull Leadership	45
The Leader's Integrity	47
Visionary and Focused Leadership	49

Leaders Care	51
Leadership Short Cuts	53
Before You Speak	55
Providing Leadership	59
Leadership Timing	61
Avoid Joysuckers!	63
Synergy Energy	65
Dummy Leadership	67
Cheer…Leaders	69
Leaders Celebrate	73
'Fit' Leadership	77
Leadership Rising	79
Light Bulb Leadership	81
Leadership Humor	83
Leadership Power	85
Change Leaders	87
How's Your Coachability?	89
Insulated or Isolated	91
Temperament Profile Leadership	93
Commanding Commitment	95
Two Great Words	97
Anonymous Sacrifice	99
Glued Open	101
A King of a Leader	105

Leadership Credit   107

Talent to Hear   109

Vunerable Transparency   113

An 18 Inch Bridge   115

Do the Right Thing   119

Rooftop Leadership   121

Honest Creativity   125

"Incite"ful Leadership   127

Best Intentions   129

What the Little Engine Teaches!   131

The Appreciation Situation   133

Butch and Leadership   135

Open Box Leadership   137

Gimli Leadership   139

'Volving' Leadership   141

Puzzling Lessons   143

I Really Appreciate You Reading This   145

Model (Car) Leadership   147

Memory Plus   149

Fast Food Leadership   151

Personal Best Leadership   155

Pitching Leadership   157

Leader Up!   159

Little Behaviors, Big Lessons   161

One Cent Lesson	163
What was the Elephant's Perspective?	165
Eyeing Perspectives	169
3 Ways to Effective Communications	171
A Perfect Union	173
A Question Worthy of Action	175
A Winning Losing Season	179
Articulate to the Audience	181
Hearing Enough to Ask	183
Hold the Pain	185
Inutshuk Leadership	187
Leadership Tea	189
Memorial Stones	191
Nice Example	193
Presenting Your Presence	195
Relative Importance	197
Self Leadership	199
Stepping Out	201
Thank You, Second Fiddlers	203
The Action Now Ability	205
The Leader's Perspective	207
The Leader's Voice	209
Therapeutic Information	211
A Note from the Author	215

99

Quick Observations

on

Leadership

Integrity First

I remember hearing a silly question, "When is a door not a door?" The answer - "When it is ajar." Get it? So my question is when is a liar not a liar? Of course the easy answer is when he is not lying. If he has a history of lying, or even the reputation of stretching the truth from time to time, he may be telling the truth in an instance, but isn't he still a liar? He may be telling truth right now. But how do you know? I guess a liar is no longer a liar when he has established himself as a person of integrity and truth.

I caught a man in a lie, and I gave him time to confess and make corrections. But when confronted by someone else he lied, and I knew it. Again, I gave him time to set it straight. He didn't. I finally confronted him. He apologized and said he was sorry. Could I trust that? He had already established himself as a person who would lie for convenience and self-promotion. How could I trust that he was sorry and would set it right? Could I trust him to set it right without lying about it? He said I could trust him. Was that a lie? Once a person has breached trust, at what point is trust re-established? How long does it take to grow integrity?

Leadership is about being trustworthy. Leaders must have integrity. If integrity is destroyed, so is the leadership. A leader may continue to dominate, manipulate or be in front, but s/he will no longer be trusted or respected. Respect will be replaced by resentment and destruction.

How long does it take to grow integrity? Leadership is built one moment at a time and on layer upon layer of honesty. How long does it take to destroy integrity? One slip of the tongue, a conscious straying and one moral or ethical line is crossed. It's so much easier to maintain integrity than get it back. The leader's first responsibility is to the truth, to maintain and build integrity.

NOTES

Customer Service is

Customer Serving

The other day I needed to do a presentation for a group. The subject was, "3 Keys to Becoming the Right Person". As I prepared the address I had an idea; how about giving each of the people a hotel room key and a marker so they could write the three main points on the plastic key? Easy Idea. But could I get the material?

First I went to the hotel desk. My thought was that maybe those keys wear out and they would have some they were throwing away, but I needed thirty! All I could do was ask. The hotel staff were fantastic. They cringed a little. I understood. But then the clerk promptly counted out thirty keys, rubber banded them together and handed them to me.

Then, I went into their small convenience shop. They had one pen that would work, and it was $2.20 (too much!). One of the staff who had heard about my idea brought me 30 markers from their store room and said they would sell them to me at a greatly reduced rate.

3

She asked how long I would be staying at the hotel. When I told her I was leaving to return to St. Louis later that day she gave me the shuttle schedule and offered to reserve me a seat. That afternoon, I ran late and once again she came to my rescue and called me a taxi. It was no problem, she said.

Customer service? You bet! These people had learned well. They were given authority to make decisions and the responsibility to carry them out. Two lessons I learned from the experience - First, they had been given the responsibility to serve the customer, along with the authority to make decisions in the moment to make a positive difference. Next, whoever trained them did a great job preparing them to serve the customer with confidence and pride for their institution.

Professional leadership - the people were trained to be a service to the customer. Personal leadership - the hotel staff exercised responsibility with authority. Another great Hilton experience.

NOTES

Private Leadership is Revealed Publicly

I met an author today who wrote a book I truly benefitted from and enjoyed. The book was on customer service, but it really went beyond that. The content was a great reminder of the right way to treat the people you work with, work for, and just come in contact with day to day.

Here's what happened. I introduced myself with a sense of anticipation. I wanted to tell him how much I really enjoyed and profited from his work. I wanted to carry on a brief but intelligent conversation about the things he communicated. I expected to have a great experience because I already knew from his writings that he would treat me as someone special.

I was wrong; he was not friendly. He asked my name and autographed the book, but barely made eye contact. I felt like I had been an imposition to him. He wrote about friendliness, but what I experienced was a contradiction. Hmmmm... It reminded me of a quote attributed to Dave Barry, "A person who is nice to you, but rude to the waiter, is not a nice person."

5

Considering leadership, it's not what you write. Neither is it what you publicly teach. It's not the aura you try to display. It's not who you portray to 'important' people. It is not even how those who are the point of your affinity feel about you. The absolute truth is that who you are in private determines your leadership in public. The foremost determination of the greatness of your leadership is how you treat people from whom you have nothing to gain.

NOTES

Passion, Enthusiasm and

Leadership

I was getting into a taxi to head for the airport in Dallas when a man asked if he could share the cab. "No problem, I'd love to have the company," I replied. He got in and we exchanged introductions and business cards.

He's a college soccer coach and was in Dallas for a youth soccer program. From there he was headed to Portugal to help their national team prepare for the World Cup matches. After a week in Portugal he was going to Germany. He would travel on to Ireland to recruit for the Portugal team. He would then travel to Portugal and finally back to Connecticut by the end of the month. He was very interesting and well-traveled!

He was passionate about soccer. But he was also interested in me. He does a fair amount of speaking on soccer and was interested in my thoughts on public speaking. We had a great conversation. He's never had any formal training in presentation skills. But he never has any trouble with speaking publicly because he loves talking about soccer. When I told him his passion and excitement probably made up for any challenges he

7

might have in his presentations, he was amazed.

Often our leadership potential is thwarted by our fears. Where we have passion we may just be a budding leader.

NOTES

Two Different Displays of Leadership

I was about to board a flight from St. Louis to Chicago. I had checked in, checked my bag, made it through security and was at the gate. Then I realized I'd left a file folder on the check-in counter. I went to the gate and let the person at the counter know of my problem. She informed me the plane was delayed and I had lots of time to go back and retrieve the folder. I probably looked pathetically at her and said, "All the way back to the check in counter, and back through security?"

Without saying a word, the gate attendant picked up the phone and called the check in counter, she confirmed they were holding my precious file folder. With a rather perturbed tone, she asked if they could meet me at security to exchange the folder. While that was a better option for me, the attendant acted as if she was really going out of her way to make the request.

I couldn't hear the entire conversation, but the person on the other end of the line offered to bring the folder all the way to the gate. When the attendant said it wouldn't be necessary, but I would meet them - I was

9

amazed. The check-in counter person, perhaps better trained in customer service, insisted they would bring it to me. I couldn't believe the attendant had tried to talk them out of it.

The counter person insisted and the gate attendant relented. She hung up the phone. With total disregard for me, she said it would be delivered to the gate. "Make sure you check in before getting on the plane." She added. I watched and watched, wanting to thank the counter person publicly, but I never saw them.

A couple of plane delays later my mind rambled onto something else; I was interrupted by the attendant. She was putting the folder between me and my book. I graciously thanked her. She didn't respond, she just walked off silently.

Which of these two people displayed leadership? Well, I guess they both did in their own way. Who would I choose to follow? (What about you?)

The first quality of leadership is personal leadership, being a person of character and credibility. One person didn't show it. She would have made me reluctant to fly that particular airline again. The other demonstrated an attitude and character that would have endeared me to the airline, (except for the context of the event). Now I'm torn. I do hope that the counter person who went out of their way for me, winds up employed at my preferred airline. Since I'll never know, I'll have to trust it to happen.

Oh well, maybe the counter person will read this and know it was them. (It was the red folder with a paper stapled on the outside). Thank you. I hope to live up to the standard you set and mimic the high quality you displayed.

NOTES

Craig S. Wagganer

Following Directions

I am in the shoe department and my wife calls. She asks where I am. I tell her. She replies that she's just left there. But maybe there are two shoe departments? She asks what floor I was on. The middle level, so that's where she goes to find me. She calls back. She can't find the shoe department on the middle level. It must be the lower level – my mistake. She gets off the escalator and heads in the opposite direction. She still can't find me. I made my way to the escalators and tell her to meet me at the up escalator. She says she is standing there. We can't see each other. Then she asks a remarkable question, "What store are you in?"

I am sure there's a lesson on communication and leadership in here somewhere. I'll use it as an illustration in the future.

I saw some children playing that old game, 'Follow the Leader'. What an interesting, insightful game! Some of the leaders were taking their followers up and down slides, onto playground equipment, around the ball diamond, then back to the playground. Others were trying to trick their followers by attempting dangerous feats, or trying to move so fast that the followers couldn't

13

Craig S. Wagganer

keep up. There was a visible difference in the kids' attitudes depending on the leader they were trying to follow.

Lots of lessons here. The children were given the task to follow and they did. It was clear to see some of the leaders were a joy to follow, while others created dread and disappointment. Part of great leadership is having people choose to follow willingly. They enjoy the journey because of the leader. Those who are forced to follow can end up regretting the effort.

NOTES

A New Word for

Leadership?

I read that about 10,000 new words get added to the dictionary each year. We need to come up with a new word for leadership. I've heard it defined as simple as leadership is influence. But there are also much lengthier descriptions.

One I like is that leadership is defined not by the leader, but by the followers. The problem is there needs to be a better word to describe great leadership. Just an understanding that the word leadership "influences" doesn't mean it's good or credible. OR (The word leadership doesn't infer its influence is good or bad (positive or negative). Many leaders have followers, which makes them leaders – in a sense. It doesn't address being responsible, or whether that leader even deserves followers. It just says leaders have followers.

Maybe a new word could mean good, credible, responsible leadership, without using so many words. Maybe we should learn to use the word leadership in a more responsible way - so that good is implied by the usage of the word. Then negative leadership could be renamed as something

15

else. Language is an interesting thing. So is leadership – good or bad.

NOTES

Leadership Humor

I was on a flight the other day and the captain was wearing a Speedo. I didn't see him, but that's what the flight attendant said. "When fastening your seat belt make sure it is tight and low across your hips like the Speedo the captain is wearing," to be exact.

That little bit of humor endeared me to the flight attendant. She'd taken a rather mundane, repetitious speech and given us a brief smile. Her light-hearted and friendly safety announcement had several humorous additives. It was fun and communicated the point. There was something in her voice that was amusing, but also revealed she was in control. In the case of an emergency, I think she'd developed enough rapport with us so we would have been comfortable following her instructions.

As we got ready to deplane, she dismissed us with a reminder to be good to one another. I sat back. How sad we have to be reminded. How important that we were reminded.

As I left I shook her hand and thanked her, she taught me another lesson in leadership. Good natured humor builds relationships and gentle reminders are helpful.

Craig S. Wagganer

NOTES

A Leader's Reflection

I hate mirrors. They show me exactly what I look like. I wish they'd lie a little. I was in a hotel room recently that had a magnifying mirror. I came close to deciding to never leave that room, or to being seen ever again. What a humiliating experience. It's bad enough to see my own reflection, but to see it magnified is just plain cruel.

But really, in a way, it's a leader's responsibility to constantly reflect, to examine things closely and take responsibility for direction. Leaders must be thoughtful in planning and execution and willing to evaluate to make sure 'it' is "right".

A good mirror is one that reflects the soul. It even magnifies so one can look intently, to see the flaws then correct the mistakes. Too often leaders are just marching forward, accomplishing the task. It's full speed ahead; we can count the bodies left in the wake later. When we reach the top of the mountain, then we can look back and see who didn't make it. Our casualties don't really matter, some of us made it. I'm not sure that is true leadership. Maybe just manipulation?

Craig S. Wagganer

Positive leadership looks forward and looks back in necessary reflection.

NOTES

Leadership from the Birds

My grand-daughter and I were at a The World Bird Sanctuary just west of St. Louis, MO. They have some great birds and wonderful venues from which to birdwatch. It was fascinating. You could see the birds up close, listen to their calls and see the splendor of the varieties of colors, sizes and physical differences. At one point, we stood in front of a wire-fenced area containing several bald eagles sitting majestically. They watched everything around them that was moving. I remarked to my grand-daughter how wonderful and amazing these great birds were. I looked over at her. She'd picked up a couple of rocks from the trail and was completely lost in the wonder of them. Here were all these fantastic birds and she was looking at paving rocks – I mean really!

Then it hit me. I walked over, bent down and picked up a few rocks. I talked with her about what she liked about them. Could I have tried to interest her in the birds? That's what had caught my attention and was why we had come there.

21

But at that point, her interest was in the rocks. So we talked about rocks for a few moments and threw a couple down into the surrounding woods. I tickled her and she tickled me back. We had a couple laughs. Then an owl hooted and got her attention. We were off to find the outspoken owl. We were back on track in what I called 'Fowl Territory'.

Leadership means knowing the goal and the direction. It's also taking time to let people experience their own interests before you guide them back on track. Time off track can often be the most important part of the journey. It may even provide important input and insights to get everyone further toward the goal.

To demand immediate or constant attention can frustrate others and become counterproductive. Hannah and I went to see birds and birds we saw. But we also enjoyed rocks, tender ribs and some laughs. Hannah taught me more about leadership than I learned about the birds on that day.

NOTES

Where Did I Say That?

I was leaving a nice hotel near the airport in a southern town. It was a short shuttle ride. I was alone with five workers from an airline that was going through contract negotiations. The two pilots and three flight attendants were very animated in their negativity about the contract situation and about their employer.

The ride lasted only a few minutes, but I'd been exposed to an extra 10 minutes of the negativity while waiting for the shuttle. It was quite a discussion. I was more than a little uncomfortable hearing it. My presence outside the hotel lobby and in the shuttle did little to deter the talk.

As we approached my drop off point, it got very quiet. Had they been unaware of my presence? Or did it dawn on them how their negativity may have impacted me?

The airline they represented is my second choice for travel. That hasn't changed, although I take comfort that it's a large airline. I hope I never have either of those pilots or any of the flight attendants.

It's reasonable to want happy pilots to be flying the airplanes I'm taking. The last thing I want is a pilot thinking; "I'll show those airline execs…"

Leaders must always be checking their attitudes. How it is affects their language and communication. It isn't just about being careful in what you say. It's also about where you say it, who you're saying it to, and who might be listening. When a leader expresses negativity about their company, or a situation within their company they must realize they may be spreading poison.

Their words can be much more powerful than they intend. Leaders must be in control of their attitudes and remain acutely aware of their situations, including their words.

NOTES

Pride and Joy

Dave works in a large school district in Southern California. He's an amazing man. He met me at the high school auditorium and asked if I needed any help.

I travel all over the U.S. teaching about leadership, public speaking and team building. I'm usually setting up in a hotel conference room, a corporate meeting room or within a company office. Often, I get asked if I need help. Usually half-hearted and said with a clear hope that my response will be a no.

When Dave asked if I needed help I answered positively then added an 'if you're serious' caveat for him. His response was amazing. He let me know I was in his house and he would do whatever it took for me to have a good experience.

He was not only serious, he was insistent. Soon he and three of his workers were helping me. My work went much easier and faster. I thanked him several times before he got started, in progress, and upon completion.

Afterwards, he let me know how important the school is to him. But then he added the phrase, "But I'm just a janitor," and smiled.

No. He tackled his job with pride and joy. He was very proud of his school and his work there. I mentioned how well-groomed the school was; neat, clean, in very good repair. It was very attractive and comfortable. Dave said it's his home while he is at work. He loves being able to share it with the kids who attend there. After all, they live there too, they're family. What an attitude!

Dave takes joy in his work. As we moved tables, stacked chairs, rearranged the room, unboxed bicycles, and prepared for the team building event; he never grumbled or complained.

Dave smiled and joked and enjoyed our work. His helpers respected and enjoyed working with him. They gave extra because of their relationship and admiration for him.

Dave said he was just a janitor, but Dave is an excellent leader. His quiet pride and joy impact all those who work for him and anyone who observes him in action.

I told him he may be at the bottom of the pyramid, but he is an important foundation.

Without him my event would have been more work and stress for me. The appearance of the building and facilities showed that there were people who cared.

I mentioned to the Superintendent and two administrators what a huge difference Dave had made. I told them he was a great help and inspiration to me. I hope they are thankful for Dave.

Leadership isn't a level attained. It's the demonstration of great character – whatever level you are on.

NOTES

Craig S. Wagganer

Unflappable Self-Leadership

I was recently on a Southwest Airlines flight and saw a remarkable incident. In the row in front of me, seated in the aisle seat, was a man who apparently wasn't having a great day. He complained that Southwest didn't have blankets or pillows. He complained that the flight had been delayed. He was not happy that his suitcase (the size of a steamer trunk) didn't fit in the overhead bin and had to be checked. I'm not sure what else – but he had a list grievances.

As the flight attendant came through the cabin, closing the overhead bins he took aim and fired. This attendant couldn't have handled the situation any better. She smiled and never stopped smiling. She answered the questions as positively and firmly as possible, never losing her pleasant smile. She didn't have an answer but she promised to find one. She apologized; reassured him the short delay would be made up in flight. We would reach our destination on time.

She had been attacked and she handled it with grace and charm. Then she continued to assist others without losing that smile or positive attitude. A few minutes later she

29

returned to check on the obstinate fellow. She gave him the answers as promised apologized for any inconveniences.

She displayed an important aspect of leadership. You must first be able to lead yourself before you can lead others. She'd mastered herself. In the face of conflict and confrontation she remained unflappable. Her grace, charm and lovely smile showed her self-assurance and professionalism. With self-control and self-mastery, she not only handled a delicate situation, but gave everyone who witnessed the encounter a great lesson in leadership.

NOTES

The Leadership Trickle

I was at the Southwest counter checking in for my flight and also needed to know how to cancel or change a flight for the next week. Cynthia was outrageously helpful. First, she told me how I could make changes so I didn't incur any change fees. She also explained how to apply the cancelled flight funds to another flight. Then Cynthia went out of her way. She cancelled the flight and booked another flight I hadn't had time to book myself. She was very helpful and very friendly.

Southwest seems to have great leadership that trickles down. Cynthia was hired for some reason. I guess that Southwest works to hire the 'right people'. She has the personality, character and a demeanor that makes her great for working with the public. I suspect Southwest has a good training program that gives employees the technical skills to accomplish tasks. It also enhances their people skills, so they work effectively and efficiently with their customers.

This trickle down training encourages wonderful people like Cynthia to exhibit personal leadership through the jungle of internet bookings and last-minute changes. Is Southwest a great airline? Yes. More

31

accurately, Southwest hires and trains great people. This makes Southwest a pleasure for airline travelers.

NOTES

Sting Leadership

The movie, "The Sting" was on TV the other night. I remember the first time I saw it in the theater when I was dating my wife – a long time ago. We got to the show early and before the prior showing had ended. We watched the ending of "The Sting" before we saw the beginning. It made seeing the whole movie really interesting because we knew what was coming. We were clued into the twist.

Seeing a movie like "The Sting" is fun. It's the little things that happen along the way that you may not catch until it's all revealed at the end. I like Alfred Hitchcock movies for the same reason. You get involved in the story but things aren't necessarily what they seem. It's great to see if you can see what's coming. But, knowing the twist ahead of time is also fun. It makes you more alert to the clues throughout.

Leaders have the ability to see ahead with clarity. They have a purpose and a plan. They are able to communicate clearly so others can catch the vision. A great asset for a leader is to selflessly see the end from the beginning. Then to describe the vision to their team, so everyone gets on board.

Craig S. Wagganer

NOTES

Sales and Self Leadership

I was thinking about the last car my wife and I purchased. Car shopping is an interesting experience. I went on-line and looked at several models then busily narrowed down the choices. I was taking my time doing the research with due diligence. Then pressure began.

The car we were replacing had been totaled. My wife and I were trying to decide whether to keep the car or trade it in. The hail damage was more extensive than we thought so there was no harm in checking what was out there. Then the front end started making a funny noise and the air conditioning went out. This happened in the midst of one of the hottest July's on record, (at least on my record). So we decided to find another ride.

After my casual research, it was time to get serious. We spent an afternoon driving, and decided on two. We had narrowed the choices down. Our first choice looked to be a done deal. I talked with the salesman; we had a verbal agreement contingent on some extraneous matters. It was a nice SUV. We were looking forward to having it. But the salesman thought if he met our payment we would be set. He could see our eagerness. I told him I had a bottom line, not a monthly payment requirement but he failed to give me a final price. He kept telling me he'd meet the monthly payment amount. In the end we were $750 dollars apart. This could have been overcome, but I couldn't get the salesman to understand our needs. He wouldn't listen to me.

While waiting for his final phone call, I went back online and investigated more cars. Our second choice was still in the running, but we just weren't as sure anymore. I sent out three emails about cars I'd found on-line. I mentioned I was willing to make a deal that day if we could work it out. I revealed the financial specifics: the size of the loan, amount down and trade-in value. My offers were reasonable, based on the cars. Of the three dealers where I inquired, one responded quickly. They said if I was satisfied after driving the car, they'd meet the trade in requirements. We could definitely make a deal that day.

A couple of hours later, I headed to the car dealership. It was a great experience! Everyone was professional, courteous and not the least bit condescending. The salesman responded honestly. We worked the deal. The financial person was helpful and kind (this may have been helped by an A+ credit score).

This leadership lesson is easy (and many). One salesperson was timely in responding, honest in communications, and helpful when dealing. One wasn't cooperative. Two failed to respond. Maybe the unresponsive dealers saw my offer and decided they couldn't do the deal. But I had asked for a response – regardless. I'd even instant messaged one. They said they would take the details to their manager and get back to me. They didn't.

The one who said we had a deal, and then tried to squeeze out a few more bucks was offensive. I walked away determined that I wouldn't do business regardless of the terms. If I couldn't trust the salesman how could I trust the dealership?

Leadership begins inside: self-leadership. One salesman demonstrated promptness, courtesy and integrity. He got the deal. I'll go back there first next time and ask for him by name. He did what he could do to make the sale. He probably wasn't even thinking about leadership, he was simply demonstrating it. Leadership that's integrated into character becomes the beginnings and the result of the leadership quest.

Craig S. Wagganer

NOTES

"CTV" Leadership

Having been a pastor I've officiated many weddings. One of my compatibility tests for prospective couples was the 'CTV' Test'. Simply stated means. 'Clean the Vomit Test'.

It means: if you are compatible, one of you has to be able to clean up vomit when either of you gets sick. I realized this from my own experience. My wife could. I couldn't. So, as a couple we passed the test. It has worked for over 37 years.

Recently, during one of my flights when the woman behind me needed another paper bag and the women in front also asked for one, I was sure I would be next.

The salvation was the flight attendant. She handled all of the passengers in her charge with grace and charm. She never showed frustration; she didn't display displeasure.

She was there helping these individuals while serving everyone else. She comforted those individuals who were nauseated, making sure they were doing fine. Everyone watching the situation was impressed. They commented on how well she handled her responsibilities, along with the demands of

39

two sick flyers. She accomplished it without the slightest sign of displeasure or stress. It was quite remarkable. I was so enamored that I didn't think about the illnesses.

A true sign of leadership is how pressure is handled. Like the common saying, leadership is like a teabag: you don't know what you've got until you drop it in hot water. Under pressure, leaders are formed and leadership will ultimately be displayed. A true leader must keep their wits, keep to the task, and inspire others even when... This flight attendant had it (kept it) down.

NOTES

Bee Leadership

I came across a short article on bees in an airline magazine. What a nice life worker bees have, at least in one respect. You see, they go out and gather pollen and then return to the hive. That's their job. Here's the deal; they have the responsibility to harvest the pollen and the authority to carry it out.

The worker bee can leave the hive with a duty to fulfill. He's not guided by another bee as to what direction or flower to visit. The worker leaves the hive to fulfill his own mission. Upon leaving the hive he chooses the direction(s) and plant(s) to use to accumulate the goods and complete the mission.

Bees have a great leadership system. The importance of the worker bee is vital to the group. Some would say it is programmed into the bee. That may be so. I wonder if this kind of responsibility and authority might not be programmed into people. First we give a person a responsibility, clearly outlining what is expected. Then we give them the authority to make decisions and instructions on how to make it happen. S/he might work like the bee, fulfilling the mission to the satisfaction of the team.

If they had responsibility but no authority, they would be like most humans who either resent the leadership, or rebel. Maybe worker bees do well because they have responsibility and authority.

NOTES

Leadership Participation

I did two events last week. The CEO's for both companies were present. I got to meet, interact, and observe them during the times I spent at their companies. Each event was fantastic and each point of contact said the programs exceeded their personal expectations. There was a lot of participation, lots of laughter, lots of interaction and response. Both events went better than either company's participants expected.

I could feel really good about the event and my ability to pull it off, but I realized something from observing the CEOs. A large part of the success of the programs was because the CEOs were well known and respected. The participants knew the CEOs and were comfortable around them. They demonstrated respect when these leaders were talking. They also welcomed their presence during the event.

One group had people who came from North, Central and South America. That CEO called each person by name. The other CEO talked to me about several different people within the organization who were from a particular locale where I had lived for

14 years.   Then he took time to make introductions.

The camaraderie at these events between the CEOs and the other participants revealed an important factor of great leadership. These CEOs demonstrated that they weren't just leading the team; they were a part of the team.   They are accepted and respected participants on the team. These leaders are followed not only because of their position or authority, but also out of respect and admiration;   and   in   part   for   their camaraderie.

NOTES

Push or Pull Leadership

I was working outside the other day and my extension cord got quite tangled.

I was stretching it out to rewind it when I was asked, "Hey, why are you dragging that cord down the driveway?"

My response was simply, "Ever try to push one?"

That's a good lesson in leadership. Leadership is more about pulling people than pushing them. Eisenhower demonstrated leadership with a piece of string; pull it and it will follow you anywhere, push it and it becomes a mess.

By pulling I don't mean dragging but rather developing motivation in others so they follow willingly. If people are scared into 'followship', they will only follow as long as they are scared. If they are reassured into 'followship' they will trust the leader until proven otherwise. If trust and credibility are established and reaffirmed, then the follower will trust the leader and anticipate a favorable outcome. The follower hasn't learned just to follow, s/he has learned about leadership.

45

Craig S. Wagganer

NOTES

The Leader's Integrity

I picked up a magazine in the airport, *Scientific American Minds*. The magazine was filled with optical illusions and is dedicated to the power of the mind. The magazine examines the intricacies of the mind as it sees images and makes connections and shows how easily we can be tricked.

One of the illusions is an old one. Two lines are placed next to each other, but in the center of the lines is a circle of a contrasting color. When you look at the lines they do not appear to be parallel. No matter how hard you look or study the picture, the lines appear to bow out in the middle. But when a straight edge is place along the lines they are indeed parallel.

The leader's life must have parallel lines. The private life and the public life must be the same if integrity is to exist. If the leader puts up a front by portraying one life in public and living another in private, it will all eventually catch up.

The word 'hypocrite' is said to have originated in the theatre. Actors wore masks to portray different characters; they were 'hypocrites.' Now, the word means someone who says one thing and does another. Nothing undermines leadership more quickly than hypocrisy.

If a leader's 'life lines' go in different directions, even if they are slightly skewed trust will be broken. Integrity will be lost and confidence shattered. We've all seen leaders who have suffered from less than congruent lifestyles. Politicians, religious leaders, company executives... the list goes on. It's imperative that leaders understand the importance of living with transparency. The private life is the public life. It is much easier to maintain integrity than to regain it.

NOTES

Visionary and Focused

Leadership

I was flying from St. Louis to Baltimore. I
think the elevation was about 38,000 feet.
As I looked out the window I could see what
I thought was Interstate 70 below. I
followed the interstate and wondered what
intersections I was viewing. I've traveled
that section so many times. But what was I
seeing? Upcoming was a large metropolitan
area. I studied the highways and
surrounding major roads.

Could it be Effingham? How long had we
been in the air? I couldn't discern Interstate
57. It would have taken off to the south on
the west side of Effingham. It would come
in the east side of the city from the north. I
couldn't see it.

Maybe Indianapolis? But there was no outer
belt around the city and there wasn't an
airport on the west side. What about Terre
Haute? But where is the Wabash River?
Was it there? Maybe I just couldn't see it
because it's tree-lined. I looked for the mall
that would be at an intersection on the
southwest corner: nothing. Before long the
city was behind me. I couldn't study it any

longer, but my mind continued to race, trying to figure out where we were.

Leaders see the view from 40,000 feet. As the saying goes: they see the big picture. They anticipate changes and problems that may occur. But leaders also need to be able to interpret and focus. They must be able to 'zoom in' and narrow the focus. Leaders must communicate the details as well as the big picture. Or they must identify someone who can help them do so.

Seeing the big picture and being able to communicate is so very important But so is being able to narrow it down into specific action.

NOTES

Leaders Care

I recently read an article online from a professor I had in college. He set a great example and had a great deal of influence on his students. One reason he gained respect was because he treated each student as an individual.

One day, I went to him after a class and asked him a question concerning an observation I'd made about the material being covered. We had a great conversation. He listened to my observations, questioned me about my reasoning and challenged me to continue checking out that train of thought. When he gave me the challenge I laughed! I was a father of two; working full-time; going to school full-time, and trying hard to keep up. I had no time for any 'side' interests. What he did next made a dramatic influence on my life. It is an incident I remember clearly.

He asked if I would be willing to forego the regular class assignments and continue my studies redirected toward the line of thinking and questions I'd presented in our short meeting. I was elated! He was genuinely interested in my learning. I felt like he was more interested in me than specific assignments. In fact, he was.

51

I worked harder on following my new course of study than if I had done what the syllabus required. It was worth it. He worked harder too. I've wondered how many lives he's influenced positively by caring so specifically about his students' learning.

Leadership isn't a road map every follower has to follow. Leadership cares about the followers and treats them as individuals. Great leaders care. They don't try to care, they really do care.

NOTES

Leadership Short Cuts

I was caught in traffic and true to my nature, I'd rather be moving than sitting still. I pulled off at the first exit and started to meander through the side streets finding my way. I saw some different sites, got frustrated by one way streets and was a little perturbed by long stop lights. It took longer to take the short cut than if I had just waited on the highway.

Leadership is earned, not asserted. There are no shortcuts. Leadership is a journey. To take an off ramp hoping to shortcut the process just doesn't work. Too many leaders want the position, the recognition and the authority, but just aren't ready. Instead of waiting until the right time, going through the process, learning lessons and being ready when called upon, we often try to take a shortcut.

We often try to assert our leadership for ego or personal needs. These kind of shortcuts result in our leadership ability being 'stunted'. It takes longer for us to gain the respect of our team and lead effectively.

I had an instructor in college who had a very strong personality. He enjoyed being a leader. He would definitely let you know it! He hadn't earned respect, he demanded it.

Instead of being an example, he would throw his weight around and force his position on those he controlled. His leadership was only positional. He never waited for people to respond to him as an instructor. Instead, he forcefully put his students under his thumb.

Was his leadership effective? His leadership status only lasted as long as the class. The students resented his strength and didn't respect him. They only recognized his leadership until his thumb was removed at the end of the semester.

Leaders don't demand followers. They learn and become leaders when they are right for the circumstances.

NOTES

Before You Speak

I came across some notes I'd written for a message I presented at a church a few years back. There were some good lessons for leaders noted. Leaders must 'think' before they speak.

T = truth. In communication make sure what you say is the truth. Not a stretch or exaggeration, but the plain and simple truth. The first standard to measure communication by is simply to ask yourself this question: "Is what I am saying the truth?"

H = help. Does what I have to say help the situation? I was told once that for every situation you encounter you come in bringing two buckets. One bucket has water and the other has gasoline. What becomes of the situation is the result of which bucket you choose to use. Many of us just react and don't take time to think. But a good question to ask before you speak is: "Does this help the situation?"

I = inspire. We need to ask: "Does this inspire?" Are the words I have to say encouraging? Do they inspire better actions, deeper thought and wider consideration? Will what I am about to say help me motivate people to do better? Then I can help not only the situation, but all the people involved. If I have an opportunity to inspire and encourage, I must take advantage of it. The words we say must create and stimulate better circumstances.

N = necessary. This is often overlooked – to much chagrin. How helpful would it be if we could just stop and ask ourselves, is what we are about to say really necessary? Does what I want to say really need to be said? Sure I want to say it. But is the basis of what I want to say dependent upon what needs to be said. So many times I could have improved a situation (and done away with later regrets), if I had simply stated what needed to be said. Not what I wanted to say. Unnecessary words can get me into trouble.

K = kind. The last question; "Is what I am about to say kind for everyone involved?" By saying "kind for everyone involved", I mean both those present and not present. What a great standard to cut down gossip, back-biting and useless, damaging conversation!

All of us, especially leaders, need to 'T-H-I-N-K' before we speak.

NOTES

Craig S. Wagganer

Providing Leadership

Leadership doesn't take - it provides.

I was recently privy to a meeting where the director of a business told a gathering of employees, "Here's what we need from you…" Then he talked about how great the company was, their successful recovery from the economic downturn, and about how well they were positioned for the coming years. In the end, it was all about how the individuals could contribute to make the momentum continue.

It was quite evident to many, the whole message was about how the employees could keep on giving. And, about finding creative ways for them to give even more. Repeatedly, the message was here's what you can do for us.

As I observed, from the outside, I could see many people bored with what was happening. People were getting increasingly concerned that the main theme was about what they could give and/or give up for the good of the company. The only reciprocal action was that by giving more they, the employees, could keep their jobs.

The attitude of the leadership was clear to everyone: "You're lucky to have us leading you, so show your gratitude and here's what we need you to do." It doesn't work.

I once had a supervisor interview me for a promotion. After asking me many questions about my experiences, my qualifications and my work ethic; he spent a fair amount of time telling me what he would do for me as my supervisor. He was concerned about me and how he could help my career, not just what I could do for him and the quality control department. At the close of the interview, I wanted the job. In other words, I wanted to work for him. He taught me an invaluable lesson; leaders provide. (Thanks Harold Koerper you were a great influence.)

NOTES

Leadership Timing

A couple of days ago I was talking to a young man who had recently quit his job. He had ethical problems with the standards of the company. It was refreshing to meet someone whose personal values were strong enough to question the workings of her/his employer's organization. In this instance the company was overcharging and/or double charging for services rendered and falsifying information on expense reports. When this young man became aware of the practices and was asked to participate, he chose to quit rather than compromise his integrity.

We had a great and lengthy discussion. His was not an easy position to be in. It's certainly not an easy decision to make, especially when making that decision affects your family and your income.

Some leaders cross the lines defining right and wrong. In the young man's case; the leadership of the company made a decision that was not only unethical, but illegal. All for the sake of money. Bad decision? Unethical and immoral? It was the leader's decision. This leadership had nothing to do with right and wrong: it was positional. Good or bad doesn't necessarily depend on

61

whether people will follow. Sometimes, people in leadership positions shouldn't be there. They are not ethical or good leaders. Sometimes they have (or hold) a position of authority and use it to manipulate others and/or circumstances. That is labeled leadership, but shouldn't be.

Real, authentic, great leadership is leadership that can be followed and trusted. It is true to high moral and ethical standards. It does what is right, not just what is expedient. It does what is right, not just what appears to be cost-effective. It does what is right without consideration of getting caught.

My father was always the greatest example of this important truth: "There is never a wrong time to do the right thing and never a right time to do the wrong things."

NOTES

Avoid Joysuckers!

I heard a word a few years back, I'm not sure where or when, but I've used it ever since. Joysucker. It describes of people who are not easy to be around. Someone who is constantly complaining and unloading on everyone. They rarely have a good time unless they are criticizing someone or something.

After a five-minute conversation with them, you just want to take a shower and lay down for a while. You refrain from asking how they are, because it will be a 60 minute conversation. They will tell you exactly how they are in drudging detail. You know this type of person. You may even be this type of person. I suppose we may all have our moments.

If you go to work and no one in the office asks how you are or they head in different directions; then you may be one of those people. If you get home from work and no one greets you, even the dog heads out the pet door. Beware! You may be one of those people.

Some leaders are 'joysuckers'. They take the fun out of the task and make sure others don't enjoy it either. They lead because of position. They feel that as a leader, they must throw their weight around. Then they make sure everyone they lead is oppressed by their power. They're 'joysuckers'.

Let's keep it simple – good leaders are not 'joysuckers'. They are 'joygivers'!

NOTES

Synergy Energy

There are a few words I dearly love. I love how they sound. I love what they mean. One of those words is *'synergy'*. It sounds neat and the meaning is fantastic; the whole is greater than the sum of its parts.

A few years ago at the county fair in Miami County, Ohio, I witnessed a horse pull. A friend of mine raised and worked draft horses. I think they were Belgians. They were big and so very strong. What he explained about them was quite inspiring. Each of the draft horses could pull only so much weight. But when teamed with others that amount went up by a greater number than just adding the two together.

It wasn't that each horse could pull 'X' amount; so four horses could pull 4 times 'X'. The formula was more startling than that. These figures aren't necessarily accurate, but you understand. One horse can pull 'X' amount of weight. Two horses don't pull 2 times 'X', but rather more like 2.5 times 'X'. The three together are pulling closer to what 4 horses can pull separately. The fourth horse takes the 'X'-factor up to about what 6 horses can do. And so on. You see the whole is greater than the sum of its parts.

65

Good leaders are synergistic. They get 100 % from their people. They can also get a synergistic effort from others so that the actual outcome of the team is greater than just the sum of its parts (strengths, talents, abilities, etc.). Members augment and complement each other in different ways so the team's efforts and impact are multiplied.

Good leaders don't subtract or divide team efforts but they do more than just put a team together. Good leaders bring synergy to the team so greater accomplishments happen.

NOTES

'Dummy' Leadership

I saw a ventriloquist on TV the other night. He was amazing. His ability to have a funny, witty conversation with an inanimate object was truly jaw dropping. As he continued I was so caught up in the humor that I truly forgot who was really speaking. I forgot one man was speaking both parts. The humor would have been great even if it had been two people. But when you think: this is just one guy and a 'dummy' – it was amazing!

Afterwards I thought, this is a great temptation of leadership. Have I ever been tempted to speak for others? Can leadership be in just one direction?. It's a danger to be avoided - manipulating people so that we can stick our hands up the, uh err... backs of others and control their words and movements.

Ventriloquist leaders aren't funny and neither are their conversations. They manipulate people by using their position or authority. They rarely care much about others. Many aren't even aware they are doing it. They think everyone else is the 'dummy' and they're the only ones who really understand. They believe they have a rare combination of insight and ability that makes them the perfect one to call all the shots.

Leaders don't speak for other people, unless it is to defend. Maybe it's better said that great leaders don't put words in the mouths of others. Enough said.

NOTES

Cheer… Leaders

My daughter, Annie, taught me a very valuable lesson when she was in high school. She tried out and made the cheerleading squad. Of course I was proud of her accomplishment but the lesson for me came when she started cheering. I was not into high school. In fact, I hated it more than anything before or since.

If mainstream church denominations are correct and there is a place of eternal punishment and torture – for me it would be high school. I only went to two high school events: the senior prom, (because my girlfriend made me) and graduation, (because my mom made me). So when Annie joined the cheerleading squad the following news was not necessarily good. We would be attending games to see her cheer. I'd never been to a high school game and wasn't looking forward to it.

We went to the games and I observed Annie and her cheer squad. They would cheer and cheer. Just by watching the cheerleaders, you had no idea of who was winning or losing or how tight the game was. The cheerleaders were doing their best to keep the fans involved and hopeful. If the team won, the cheerleaders were excited and led the celebration. If the team lost they were still energetic in consoling the team. They reinforced how good their effort was and how they would fare better next time.

I often observed that if the team played great and had a good game, coming out on the winning side, the crowd would congratulate the team and celebrate with them. If the team didn't play so great, or played a better team, and they lost – it was the coaches' fault. It couldn't be our kids; it must have been the coaching.

I never witnessed anyone saying if the team won, "Hey cheerleaders – you were on tonight. You really inspired the team with your motivational cheers. If it weren't for you cheerleaders we would never have won the game!" Likewise, I never witnessed anyone saying, "Wow, you cheerleaders were really off tonight. Your cheers were lackluster at best. If you would have cheered better we could have won the game." If the team won, the cheerleaders received no credit or glory. If the team lost, they received no criticism or blame. Yet, the cheerleaders were completely invested in the team.

Good leaders have a team mentality. They are completely invested in the success of the group. They recognize there is no real success without the team, and they share that concept with others. Leaders understand that a loss is not failure, but an opportunity to improve. Great leadership means being a cheerleader for the team and being completely invested in its success.

NOTES

Craig S. Wagganer

Leaders Celebrate

In my current position I often use the phrase, "people learn best when they are having fun." I really believe when you are enjoying yourself, you open up to many possibilities. When I am having fun I can easily learn lessons from what was going on. When I associate the lessons with a pleasurable experience, it reinforces the learning.

So, the best way to turn a negative experience into a positive one is to learn what lessons we can from it. Take the negative and learn as much as you can from it. Then it becomes a positive learning experience. When you're able to do that, the negative becomes an opportunity and can even be enjoyable. Not because of the experience itself, but because you will benefit from it another way. So celebrate!

Good leaders celebrate! They not only celebrate their own learning and positive direction, but they truly enjoy celebrating the success of others. A long time ago I received a note of congratulations when I received a job promotion. The note came from the supervisor I would be leaving when I took the promotion. I had a great friendship with this boss and I'd miss him. I worked hard for him. He'd shown appreciation all along the way. But when opportunity presented itself to move into another position, I was ready and able. It meant a different location and a different supervisor.

My move would temporarily put my old supervisor in an awkward position. He'd have to replace me and my job would be difficult to fill. But this leader came to me, expressed appreciation for our time together and congratulated me on my success. He gave me a congratulatory card with some heart-felt words that let me know he was proud of my growth and sincerely happy for me.

He was always like that, he celebrated with his team. There were times we met business goals, reached quotas, or simply had good results. He celebrated with us. He was aware of our personal lives and celebrated the birth of children, anniversaries and our accomplishments. Whatever we might celebrate, he noticed and he cared.

What a good and effective leader! Good leaders celebrate with their people. Good leaders make it fun. Good leaders get the party started.

NOTES

Craig S. Wagganer

'Fit' Leadership

I recently saw the movie "Gladiator" on TV. I've seen it before but I like the TV version because it cleans up a lot of the gore. The movie has some great leadership lessons. In the movie the main character begins as a leader, loses it, and then becomes a leader again.

His leadership is not pursued or desired, it is just part of his nature to be followed. The gladiator isn't looking to be a leader, but he takes the lead in his own life. Others respect him and choose to follow him. They trust him and maintain allegiance to him. They follow him out of respect and a desire to be where he is going.

This is an important characteristic of good leaders. They don't necessarily pursue leadership, but rather rise to it. Their character and passion causes others to commit to them and their cause.

Often, good leaders lead because of the circumstances they find themselves in. Perhaps it's a situation where they are called to lead because of their talent, strength, skills, or their passion to make a difference. To lead convincingly, they must have humility and confidence. They don't convince others to follow simply because they are confident. It is because there is a calling, a fulfillment. They fit the situation or position. They recognize it's not all about them; it's about what can be accomplished.

Great leaders understand their 'fit' and are humble about it - being humbled by it.

NOTES

Leadership Rising

I bought a bread mix the other day at the grocery store. I thought it would be fun to make my wife a fresh-baked loaf of bread. I read the label. All you have to do is put the mix into the bread machine, add warm water and turn on the machine. I could do that.

I don't know exactly how bread machines work. I don't know how the mix works. I do know it uses yeast. The yeast is added and has to be given time to work. Somehow the yeast permeates the whole lump of dough and causes it to rise. I'm not sure how that works. It was explained to me one time that without yeast, the loaf of bread would be a brick. The yeast makes it light and fluffy and causes all the little holes that make the bread a loaf and not a door stop.

Great leadership is like yeast. First, it takes time. Leaders rarely just become good leaders, especially the great ones. It takes time to rise – time to build experience and potential into a working team. Time is needed to learn how to take advantage of the leadership opportunities when presented. But once a leader rises, she/he also causes everything around them – especially people – to rise as well.

If a leader isn't like yeast, his leadership will be a brick and cause others to be weighed down. Here's a good test for leadership; are you growing and causing everyone around you to grow as well?

NOTES

Light Bulb Leadership

I know I can be slow, but I noticed something the other day. When I turned on a light bulb – the darkness left. I know this is not an astute observation. In fact, the reason for turning on a light bulb is to dispel the darkness. When we turn on a light it is so we can see. The room becomes illuminated. We don't really think;' I sure need to get rid of the darkness'. Instead, we think we need to see.

Someone should write a book called Light Bulb Leadership. It should be about how great leadership sheds light and takes away the darkness. So many times, I've heard people say, "I don't know what's going on, they (the leaders) always leave us in the dark until the last moment." Great leadership doesn't like darkness – for themselves or for their people. Great leadership is all about illumination.

Too often leaders cast darkness. We hold information rather than sharing it. We know information is power. To share information may empower other people and threaten our own power. So we keep information to ourselves.

Leaders also cast darkness by playing the blame game. A problem occurs and the first thing we do is try to find who is to blame rather than solve the problem. No matter the problem, an illuminating leader will try to solve the problem and not be so concerned with blame. The blame is not important. The long-term solution should be the focus. If blame is assigned and a person is the problem, the issue should be resolved in a way as to keep the person's dignity. Good leaders do this by addressing the problem behavior without attacking the person.

There are a lot of ways leaders cast darkness instead of light. But good leaders are light bulb leaders that illuminate. They shed light and remove darkness.

NOTES

Leadership Humor

Doing a couple of team building programs in the past week I witnessed something quite remarkable. On two separate occasions I saw the team leaders using humor in their communications as they interacted with their teams. The difference it made was quite startling.

One leader continually put their team on the defensive by using humor to attack. There was a lot of laughter. A lot of the things said were very witty. But the comments, although funny, created tension within the group. I'm sure the leader was just trying to be funny, but the humor was biting. Often times, it was at the expense of someone in the group. Everyone tried to take it good naturedly, but you could see damage being done.

In the other instance the team leader that used humor, was comforting and added to the team spirit. This leader was very observant. He used situations as the palette for the humor. Any cutting humor concerned only him. He was able to laugh at himself in a way that wasn't critical of the team or their efforts. The team was very much at ease. They enjoyed the laughs in a much more comfortable way.

Great leadership uses humor in a way that creates comfort, not tension.

NOTES

Leadership Power

If you get the chance see the movie "The Last Castle" starring Robert Redford and James Gandolfini. It's an interesting study on leadership. Gandolfini's character leads by intimidation and power. Redford's character leads by respect and value.

One is a military prison commander. The other, a U.S. Army General convicted of disobeying a direct order. One holds great power and wields it over everyone, from his staff to the prisoners. The other treats every man with dignity and respect. One shows his leadership by constantly being angry, wielding threats and violence. The other shows interest in each individual, appealing to their honor and values. One wins, but it costs him his life. The other loses and loses his position.

Here's the key for me; one leads by power and one leads by empowering. Leadership is not about power, it is about empowering.

NOTES

85

Craig S. Wagganer

Change Leaders

I was recently given the task of planning a team building activity designed around change. The sponsoring organization had been through significant changes and they were expecting more. Leadership wanted their people to be healed and prepared. I planned and presented a program that spoke to their situation. They were grateful for the information and the people responded favorably.

Here are some lessons I learned along the way. First, change is inevitable. (Ever heard that?). But good leaders change intentionally. They are constantly evaluating and making changes as the need arises. However, leaders don't make changes for change's sake. They change for goodness sake (pardon the cliché, but understand how it applies here). Since change is necessary good leaders make it happen with as much ease and comfort as possible, with positivity. The good leader makes clear the positive nature of any and all changes.

Next, change is inevitable so changing is also inevitable. That may sound redundant or like double-talk, but it contains truth. When change occurs good leaders adjust.

87

They make the most of any situation for themselves and especially for their people. Good leaders don't continue to be the same or expect the same from their people. Rather as change comes, the good leader changes and helps the team to understand and adjust.

Good leaders change according to need and according to their needs. Good leaders change internally and externally.

NOTES

How's Your Coachability?

Shortly after getting married, I played softball for what may have been the worst softball team in the history of the world! There were only three of us who had ever played organized ball. The rest could have been picked last in a high school gym class. The team was organized by my brother and his friends just for fun, and that it was! My brother, after getting a look at the players' abilities promptly moved to Florida after one practice.

My brother's good friend was the coach. What a horrendous responsibility. The bright spot was that we had no false hopes or dreams about being good. Our goal was to win one game. But the coach took his job seriously. He did as good a job as he could with the 'Worst News Bears'.

The greatest lesson: our coach was both a coach – and coachable. Although he was 'in charge,' he was very willing to take advice. He really listened to those who had more experience playing softball.

This is key for leaders. We must understand our coaching position. It's not our job just to get things done. We must also bring out the best in each person and respond to their strengths. This brings out the best in the team. Good leaders coach and are coachable.

NOTES

Insulated or isolated?

I recently saw the movie Mister Roberts. It stars two of my favorite actors: Jimmy Cagney and Henry Fonda. I love Jack Lemmon's character as well. The movie is about the turmoil of a crew with an unlovable commander. It is a comedy. The movie juxtaposes two leaders: Cagney's character is the commander who has authority but no respect. Fonda's character has the admiration and respect of the crew, but no (little) authority. The two roles (characters) taught me something about isolation and insulation.

Cagney's character was isolated. He didn't interact with the crew. He was the leader but only in position. No one liked or respected him. They followed his orders out of fear of possible retribution. Cagney thought there was a team, there wasn't. Although isolated from them, he was not insulated. The result was a mutiny – of sorts.

Fonda's character was insulated but not isolated. He heard the crew's complaints, commiserated with them and worked to solve problems. He didn't isolate himself. Rather he was a part of the team, even through dire circumstances. By being part of the team, Fonda's character was loved and respected. The men fought for him.

'It is lonely at the top', goes the old saying. This is true for the type of leader who isolates himself/herself from their people. The leader that associates, identifies, cares for and loves their people will be insulated from the horrors of loneliness.

NOTES

Temperament Profile

Leadership

It can be humorous to hear people talk about their own leadership. I was working with a person who declared; "If I start taking over, excuse me. After all, I'm a 'D'." She was referring to a popular personality test where she had scored high as a direct, dominant, demanding, decisive person. Since the test had revealed those prominent characteristics, it was now something she/he used to define herself/himself – and excuse obtrusive behavior. The implication is: 'After all, that's just how I am'.

Good leaders are not defined by personality or temperament categories. Good leaders are across the board in personality types, temperament styles, or any other such classifications. Tests that help us understand our propensities and reveal characteristics can be good, if they help us understand our strengths and weaknesses. But we in turn, must capitalize on our strengths and mitigate our weaknesses. If the knowledge creates self-justification for our behavior giving us excuses for what we do, it's gone from being beneficial to destructive.

Leaders who believe their qualifications for leadership come from their own personalities or temperaments usually lead from a position of power that's asserted, not earned. Followers soon become aware when a person has no real ability to lead. Then they generally quit following - if they have a choice. If the followers are not in a position to quit, they simply lose respect and grow resentful towards the leader. A leader in that situation is usually the last to know when problems exist. If he/she is aware there are problems with the team, they often attribute it to the personalities of others, rather than their own leadership inabilities.

NOTES

Commanding Commitment

I heard an interesting comment the other day. It wasn't really a comment it was a command. The CEO of a company said; "We don't just expect total commitment from our employees; we demand it." I'm sure many employees aren't committed, even if they look like it. That's the interesting thing to me. Leadership may demand total commitment, but with that attitude I'll bet they get very little.

Total commitment must be inspired. It cannot be commanded. When a leader commands, it breeds resentment and frustration. There's nothing more annoying to most people than having something demanded of them, especially when it should be cultivated. Demanding commitment is like ordering something at a restaurant: you may get what you ordered, but if you irritate the server, you may not. Worse yet, you may get what appears to be your order, but with additional ingredients.

Leaders who demand commitment, or anything else, are asking for trouble. They get what appears to be commitment, but really it's more like compromise. Compromise can look like what the leadership ordered, but it has added ingredients like resentment and sabotage. I'm not talking about outright destruction, but about doing small things that violate the company. Small things may go unnoticed for the moment, but they show up later as diminished morale (or other problems).

Great leaders inspire and cultivate commitment. Their concern for the organization, especially its people, is an example of their own commitment. Inspiration and cultivation are modeled through relationships. Positive commitment is inspired and cultivated by great leaders who care.

NOTES

Two Great Words

I came across a little piece of paper that I'd written two words on. Both words are Japanese. One word is from a Peter Drucker book. (but I don't remember which one). Luckily, I had the definitions of both words written down. I have a couple of reminders about their meanings. The words are great leadership words.

The first word is 'Kaizen'. I have written with it 'continuous improvement'. Great leaders are committed to continuous improvement. But they put into practice 'kaizen'. It doesn't mean they are never satisfied. They are committed to innovation and continuously looking for ways to improve themselves and their situations.

The second word is from the Drucker book. The word is 'Kieretsu'. The meaning I have written is: 'ownership from beginning to end'. Great leaders own the process from beginning to end. The word refers to companies that operate the entire process of their product manufacturing. An example of the process would be like this: the company would operate the mining of raw materials, then refine and process the materials. Then the company would create and assemble the parts (from the raw materials). Finally they

97

would market and sell their product. (They 'own' the entire process.)

Great leaders own the process from beginning to end. Their successes are the team's. The failures are learning experiences for the leader. Great leaders own the process and take the ultimate responsibility. Successes are shared. Failures are absorbed.

Great leaders are tremendous performers of 'kaizen' and 'kieretsu' maybe without ever knowing the words or their meanings. Continuous improvement and ownership are important qualities for every leader to develop.

NOTES

Anonymous Sacrifice

A couple of years ago my wife and I were returning to St. Louis from Baltimore. She had been reading, then she shut her book. She closed her eyes and put her head on my shoulder. I love the fact that we are still affectionate after 38 years of married life. But after having her head on my shoulder for a few minutes it began to hurt.

There's some long medical term for the problem in my neck. I'm not sure what it is, but it causes pain in my shoulder and down to my wrists. The longer her head was on my shoulder the greater the pain. Although I was increasingly more uncomfortable, I didn't move or disturb her. If she actually fell asleep, I knew we'd be landing in less than an hour. After a few minutes she raised her head and opened her book again, never knowing of my discomfort.

Caring relationships are good examples of leaders. Leaders take pain for those they lead. Their compassion causes them to care. Great leaders sacrifice for what and who they care about. They put their own comfort behind the needs of others. If anyone else had put their head on my shoulder, I would have excused myself, explained the pain and repositioned. But it was my wife. I'm willing to take the pain as long as necessary for her to be comfortable.

Great leaders are easy to follow. Their sacrificial attitude makes them easy to follow. They show their followers they care about them. It's not to draw attention to themselves or about the sacrifices they make. Great leaders sacrifice and keep quiet about it.

NOTES

Glued Open

I was reminded of an event that happened years ago. I was at a card shop with my wife and my mother. I watched them laughing so hard they were wiping tears away. Of course I wanted to get in on the hilarity but when I approached them they were both laughing so hard they couldn't let me in on the joke. They just handed me the card they thought was so funny.

It was a birthday card. On the outside the card said something like; "When we were young we used to pull pranks on each other, play practical jokes and trick and tease each other. But now that we're grown, isn't it great we can have a mature, respectful relationship? So on your birthday, I just wanted to let you know..." With that, you're supposed to open the card to finish reading the sentimental conclusion – but the card is glued shut.

Of course when I made my attempts to open the card, it sent my wife and mother back into hysterics.

What had happened that I didn't know was my mother had picked up the card first and spent a great deal of time trying to open it before she finally got it. She laughed out

101

loud. My wife came over to her and mom handed her the card. My wife tried to open it and couldn't. Which, of course, made my mother laugh harder. Then when my wife finally 'got it', she laughed at the card and laughed harder that my mom was laughing.

You know how that goes? The laughter is contagious. They couldn't stop. It was dying down when I had my experience with the card, but then the laughter started over again.

Things had about settled down when one of us - I'm not sure who - said we were going to write a book called, Everything I Know About Sex and Am Not Afraid to Tell. The book would be glued shut. More laughs! We didn't buy the card and the book hasn't been published.

What does this have to do with leadership? I've known leaders who were closed books. Their lives were secretive and solitary. They were not open, so their leadership (and motives) were always in question.

Great leaders are open books. Their life is one of character and credibility. They may have made mistakes - big ones. But their mistakes aren't hidden or ignored. Their mistakes are dealt with; lessons are learned

102

and growth happens. Great leaders are open books.

NOTES

Craig S. Wagganer

A King of a Leader

I caught just a part of a news report on a new Martin Luther King, Jr. Memorial. It piqued my interest. I went to my book shelves and found a little book I'd recently picked up on his speeches. I began reading, hit and miss, here and there, just looking at snippets of what he said. I was fascinated. It was great reading. I was in awe as I remembered he'd written all these words and made all of these speeches. The words were inspiring to read. How much more powerful it must have been to hear those words spoken.

I'm certainly not an expert on MLK by any stretch. I remember him. I remember when he was shot. I remember there were critics and fans. But the more I learn about him and read his words; the more of a hero he has become for me.

He was a great leader. Great leaders communicate passion and inspire action. Note: there is a subtle but important difference between communicating with passion and communicating passion. Dr. King could do both. But he was most effective because he communicated passion. Of course there needs to be a caveat, the passion inspired must be for the good and the resulting action must be good. King did that.

I deeply respect a person who can so effectively communicate and change minds for the better. I don't mean brain-washing, coercion or manipulation. Rather, someone who is so passionate about a cause that is right, just and good. They communicate in such a way as to change people. The result is what is best for everyone. Martin Luther King, Jr. was able to do that.

Good leaders communicate passion and inspire action.

NOTES

Leadership Credit

I saw a great T-shirt recently. It simply stated, "Which way did they go? I must follow them, I'm their leader!"

What a great leadership attitude! Leaders are team players. Their success is a team accomplishment, not an individual reward.

Every leader needs to recognize the people who have gone before and paved the way for them. Leaders owe a debt of gratitude to those who are supporting them and working with them. They also need to recognize those who will take the torch and carry on.

A great leader is always behind their team.

NOTES

107

Craig S. Wagganer

Talent to Hear

I met my friend near Washington DC for supper. We entered the restaurant and the greeter showed us to our table and let us know that Angela would be our server. Angela would be with us momentarily. A few seconds later a young lady approached our table. As she was walking our way I smiled a big smile and said, "Hi Angela, how are you this evening?"

The young woman stopped. She looked quizzically, then said, "Do I know you? Have you been here before?" Then she asked, "Have you been at another restaurant where I work?" And then came the one I usually get when I do this, "Do you know my parents?"

I apologetically stated, "I am so sorry. I didn't realize I called you by name. I am so sorry. Ever since I was a child I've had the ability to look at someone and know their name. I get an immediate impression and it's 99% accurate. When you approached the table the impression was so strong that I called you by name and didn't even realize it. If I embarrassed you, please forgive me."

Angela said with amazement, "That's fantastic, I've never met anyone who could do that!" My friend, who has known me all his life responded, "I didn't know you could do that. That's fantastic. Why didn't you ever tell me you had this power?"

I downplayed it as much as I could. I asked if they would just forget about it. "This time was an accident. Could we just forget it and go on with the meal."

We did and it was an enjoyable meal with excellent service. I drink decaf coffee and my cup never got less than half full. Angela made sure everything was fine. She refreshed our water; brought us more bread and butter – whatever we needed, or she thought we needed.

When we paid for the meal, Angela told us what a pleasure it was to serve us. She said if we were ever in the area again please come back and ask for her by name. Angela said she'd never met anyone like me.

So now it was my confession time. "Angela, you need to know that I don't have any special powers or insights. Sarah, the greeter, said our server would be Angela. That's how I knew your name. That's all."

Angela's response, "No. No. You can do it. I know you can do it."

My friend chimed in, "You can do it. You said you don't like to draw attention to it and now you're just trying to cover it up. You really can do it." Angela continued to nod in agreement.

After a few minutes of arguing I finally put my foot down. I stated emphatically the only way I knew Angela's name was because the greeter had told us. "End of story." I said. "Sarah said our server would be Angela. When you approached the table I said your name because Sarah had told us."

My friend's response, "I didn't hear her say that!"

My response, "You weren't listening."

A major factor in leadership is listening. Too many leaders just want to be listened to, but great leaders develop the skill of listening. Good listening is more than just waiting your turn or thinking about your response while someone else is finishing their statement. Good listening is paying attention to the speaker and making sure you hear what they are saying. We filter out what we don't think is important: what the greeter says, what the store clerk offers, the flight attendant's instructions, the cab driver's conversation. There are too many to mention. But it also includes our co-workers, friends and family.

Great leaders understand it's more important to listen than to talk.

NOTES

Vulnerable Transparency

There's an old card playing phrase I'd not heard for a long time. I heard it used recently to characterize a leader. Two people were apparently discussing their leadership and one said to the other, "They sure hold their cards close to their chest. I sure wish I knew what they were thinking."

There are times when great leaders must practice confidentiality. But great leaders also share their hearts. They are open and honest about themselves and the situations around them. They have a transparency that helps people see and understand their heart. People understand and know where they stand. It's not a forthright telling of opinions but rather an honest and open character who risks vulnerability for the sake of being understood. These leaders aren't afraid to open up. They realize that team building and follower building is a matter of the heart, not just the brain.

It may be a fine line, but great leaders learn it and practice transparency. Great leaders share their hearts, they don't guard them.

NOTES

Craig S. Wagganer

An 18 Inch Bridge

I attended a meeting where there was a hotly debated topic. The issues were large. There appeared to be a lot at stake. There were clearly two sides.

One group had logic and clear thinking on its side. But emotions were running high. The logical group kept calm and collected as they presented the reasons why the issue should be decided in one direction. The emotional group had no supporting evidence but they kept getting louder and louder.

It was an amazing thing. As the emotional leader increased volume, it intimidated people. The logical group's arguments were clear and made sense. The emotional group was clear, but had no real support other than to sway people by using loud voices – which they did. In the end the vote went the emotional way. Within two weeks everyone regretted the decision.

The decision was final, and the emotional leader 'got his way'. There was no way to go back. That decision became the undoing of the organization.

I saw two important lessons. The first: to sway people you have to connect to their emotions. Logic is good and necessary, but it can be more convincing when it appeals to emotions. The best communicators recognize this and appeal to people with data supported by stories. Information must connect to the heart to be convincing. There must be an 18 inch bridge from the head to the heart if facts are going to convince people and make a difference.

The other lesson is that great leaders are not the loudest voice. Rather they facilitate the best dialogue. In the meeting there was one side that got louder and louder. They did not discuss, but accused. They had no supporting evidence; instead they attacked the differing viewpoint. The ungrounded accusations did plant the seed of doubt. They began to intimidate people. To stand opposed would risk ridicule and possible embarrassment. The loud voice was very intimidating. It won.

The loudest voice won, but the organization lost. The decision split leaders apart. The CEO and several ranking officers left. The organization suffered and has not recuperated.

Great leaders take responsibility. They connect the head and heart, they don't just sway the heart. Make certain that the loudest voice comes from a true leader.

116

Great leaders don't intimidate and they aren't necessarily the loudest voice. They do facilitate the best dialogue. Great leadership is about dialogues – not monologues.

NOTES

Craig S. Wagganer

Do the Right Thing

At a gathering of men a few years ago we were discussing our parenting. We each were asked to narrow down one or two things we learned from our fathers. For each of us it was not easy. There are so many lessons learned from dads.

After much thought and much discussion, I narrowed my response down to one thing… Dad taught me that there is never a right time to do the wrong thing or a wrong time to do the right thing.

Dad taught me that self-control and integrity are of the utmost importance. The wrong thing is always the wrong thing – don't make excuses or allowances. The right thing is always the right thing – do it.

We'll bury dad this afternoon. But the light of the truth he taught me and displayed throughout his life will continue to shine. I pray I might be worthy to be remembered for the same thing.

My dad taught me the most important part of leadership, leading yourself.

Craig S. Wagganer

NOTES

Rooftop Leadership

My mother had a saying that has echoed to me across the years. One of her favorite sayings; "Better safe than sorry". I specifically recall this admonition concerning one temptation that was recurring to me.

My mother's parents lived next door to us when I was growing up. The only things separating the two houses were double driveways. At the top of each driveway was a garage.

My grandparents' garage had a flat roof and ours was pitched. I'm not sure of the pitch, but it was scary steep. The garages were connected by a chain link fence that bridged the short gap between them. I remember the gap as a much larger chasm, but in reality it was about 3 feet.

My mother always warned me about climbing on the garage roofs. Better safe than sorry. Better not climb up there and take any chances that you will fall and get hurt. She also let me know (with no uncertainty) that if I made the climb and fell; the pain of disobeying would be worse than being injured from the abrupt stop at the end of the fall.

But the garage rooftops were so inviting. From the top of the fence you could jump up and catch the flat part of my grandparents' garage. Then it was easy to pull yourself up and then make the leap over to the pitched roof. You had to be careful. There was some trepidation, but leaning forward to fall onto the pitch made for a successful attempt. Not that I would know, but I can imagine.

I also imagine that the only close call would come if my brother, at the coaching of his friend, would throw a ball over the roof at the precise moment of an otherwise perfect leap. All of this conjecture, mind you. I'd never admit to it actually happening.

Great leaders have a high risk-reward threshold. They usually are higher risk takers than most.

We all know experience is the best teacher. That has changed in recent years to someone else's experience is the best teacher.

Great leaders take risks so they can learn and share the lesson. They take risks knowing the experience will make them smarter and stronger, all the while helping others to learn.

NOTES

Craig S. Wagganer

Honest Creativity

Original creativity is invaluable; just ask those of us that don't have it. We marvel at people who have great ideas. We wonder where they came from and why we didn't think of ...whatever. Truly creative people are a treasure.

I've been very envious of the creative people. Then I learned about the second type of creativity – borrowed creativity. These are people like me. We have developed the ability to seek out creative people and capitalize on their talents. I'm not too creative but I do have a small streak. I work at being creative, it doesn't come natural. I've learned to look for creative people and creative resources. Then I borrow from them and use their creativity to my benefit and to benefit those around me.

People have flattered me by saying that I'm creative. I correct them whenever I hear it. Others have asked me how I became so creative. I tell them the truth – I borrowed it. When people come up to me and say that my idea was great, I acknowledge that it is a great idea, but I may not be exactly sure who or where the idea came from. A quote I love is; 'The art of creativity is the ability to forget your source'. I've borrowed creativity

125

but I try to give credit when and where it is due. My creativity is being able to seek out the creative around me.

Great leaders are creative, whether they are originally creative or they are 'borrowers'.

NOTES

"Incite"ful Leadership

One of my favorite movie lines comes from the great western, The Magnificent Seven. Steve McQueen's character is asked why they would come to defend a small town against tremendous odds. His reply is something like; "It's like the guy who took off all his clothes and jumped naked into a bed of cactus. I asked him why he did it and he said it seemed like a good idea at the time."

Leaders take the first step. That doesn't mean they are reckless or do things without thinking, but rather when they are convinced it's time to take action, they do. They move when others are watching, waiting or encouraging someone else to do the task. Leaders may misstep, they may fall, or they may not end up with a good decision after all. But when it is time to move, they move. Many people stand around observing and reporting. They can look at a situation, then try to coerce others into action. Leaders don't push others to act if they are unwilling. Leaders will take the risk themselves instead of putting someone else in harm's way.

Great leaders facilitate action. They take the first step. Great leaders don't take action to brag, to benefit themselves or receive glory.

127

They act because it is right, necessary and best for all involved. They step up and they step out. They facilitate those around them to greater actions. They see themselves as serving the greatest need, not seeking the greater glory.

Great leaders are action-oriented and facilitate the actions of those around them.

NOTES

Best Intentions

I wonder how many times I've said, either out loud or to myself, "I was only trying to…" You know the situation. You were trying to do something good. You had great intentions but it didn't turn out as planned. You tried to explain what you were thinking and how your motives were good, but it just didn't turn out the way you expected.

Great leaders have good intentions; it just doesn't always work out the way they desired. Here is a safeguard for testing those good intentions. Consider what is BEST for all concerned. Be aware of how the decision and resulting actions will affect everyone, even remotely involved in the outcome.

Consider what is BEST for all concerned:

Benefit – Think win-win as Stephen Covey encourages. Don't accept anything less. If it isn't obvious, then take the difficult step of continuing to work it out. Don't do what's easiest, but what benefits everyone concerned.

Encourage – Make sure the decision and resulting actions move people and situations forward. Make sure encouragement is part of the plan. We need to look at what we are

129

doing and frame it so it builds people up and doesn't tear them down. A good barometer of how good your intentions are: evaluate how it will build others.

Stimulate – Our intentions, decisions and actions should stimulate others to follow. Not in an arrogant "look at me" or "do as I do" attitude, but rather by setting a good example. Others should see our decisions and actions, the results of our good intentions and imitate them. We should stimulate others in productive and creative ways.

Tangible – the end result of our good intentions should be tangible. Our intentions, decisions and resulting actions should provide a substantial experience for everyone involved. That experience should be one that's a profitable benefit and offers concrete assistance to everyone.

Great leaders provide what is BEST for all concerned.

NOTES

What the Little Engine Teaches!

One of my wife's favorite children's books is "The Little Engine That Could". You know the story; the little train engine was faced with a log steep hill and needed to get over it. The engine keeps telling himself, "I think I can, I think I can, I think I can..." Then he does!

It is a great story about self-confidence, believing in yourself, and giving it all you've got. Of course leaders have these qualities. But great leaders go a step beyond. It's a wonderful thing to have belief and the confidence in yourself to do more than expected. But great leaders have that and a belief in others.

One secret to great leadership is developing more leaders. It's more than just thinking you can, it's developing that same attitude in others. It's great to say, "I think I can, I think I can, I think I can..." But is it better to say, "I know you can, I know you can, I know you can..."

At the end of the children's book the little engine that could did. Then he proclaimed, "I knew I could!" But great leaders get a

131

deeper satisfaction from teaching others to believe in themselves. Great leaders take people from hearing, "I know you can, I know you can, I know you can..." to "Congratulations, you did it! I knew you could!"

NOTES

The Appreciation Situation

For some reason I was thinking about my daughter-in-law's birthday. She's a wonderful woman, a fantastic mother, and a quality human being in every way. She is full of faith, grace and is a joy to be around. She and my son are growing kids that are a funny, creative, intelligent and a real pleasure. I'm not just saying that because they are my grandchildren – it really is true!

One of the nice things about the way we celebrate birthdays is a tradition my son, Zac, started in recent years. After the birthday meal, after the candles are blown out, but before we eat the cake, or pie, or special dessert; we take time affirm the birthday celebrant. It isn't just a compliment; it goes deeper than that. We take time to go deeper and explain an attribute we've observed and really appreciate about that person. Some call it a 'strength-centered compliment'.

It's as simple as this, "I really appreciate (insert name) and the reason I say that is…"

Our grandchildren are being steeped in this family tradition that my son wisely began. It's a very valuable time for both the giver of the compliment and the receiver.

Great leaders show appreciation, are generous with compliments but they go a little deeper. They help build character qualities by acknowledging the strengths of their team members. They give out character affirmations in front of others.

NOTES

Butch and Leadership

One of my favorite movies is *Butch Cassidy and the Sundance Kid*. I just about have about the whole movie memorized. There are some great quotable lines. One of the best is when the main characters are heading back to the hide out. Butch shares an idea of going to Bolivia. After talking back and forth, Butch makes the statement; "I've got vision where the rest of the world wears bifocals."

Butch displayed a great component of leadership – vision. Vision is the ability to innovatively look into the future and to see what needs to be accomplished. It begins with passion and leads to action. Everything great that's been accomplished began with vision.

Are all great leaders visionaries? No. Many great leaders were visionaries, but that isn't necessarily a primary component. Great leaders act on the vision, even if the vision comes from another. Great leaders are action-oriented. They take time to think things through. They evaluate tangents and see the big picture. They are more than visionaries because they act on the correct expedient vision.

135

The Biblical King of Israel, David had a vision. He wanted to build a house for God – it drove him. He wanted to do this for the God he served and the God who had delivered him so many times. He had the vision. It was his son, Solomon that brought it to pass. It wasn't Solomon's vision – it was his father's. David began accumulating all the materials for the Temple and the interior furnishings; but under the leadership of Solomon the Temple was started and completed.

Vision is a fantastic quality possessed by a precious few. But discernment and action earmark great leaders.

NOTES

Open Box Leadership

I was going about my task doing a team building event. It was a large event. There were a lot of bikes to unpack from their boxes. The usual process is to open the top reach down inside the box and remove part by part. There had to be a better way. I had a box cutter, so I decided to lay the box down flat and cut out the side. I could expose the whole bike and the various parts. Then I could close the box back up so it could be taken away.

It really wasn't a great innovation, but it made the job easier and more efficient. The shame of it was, (I have to admit), is that it took me quite a while to come up with the idea. The old process of ripping the box top that was stapled and glued, then working to get everything out of the box, was much more difficult. But I'd learned the process one way and never questioned it.

Great leaders challenge the process. They look for better, more efficient, effective ways to accomplish a task. It could be simple. It can be very involved and difficult. But the process is always open for consideration. Too often, the process isn't open for consideration. Because it's viewed as being owned by the person who invented it. If we challenge 'the process', we are challenging the inventor.

Poor leaders guard the process, (because of ownership). Great leaders challenge the process they know the results are important. Progress is important – more important than ego and ownership.

It's been said before, the seven last words of a dying organization, "We've never done it that way before".

NOTES

Gimli Leadership

The *Lord of the Rings* movie trilogy is very popular. There is a scene in one of the movies where a dwarf and his friends are confronted with an impossible situation but they knew they had to continue their journey. The character, Gimli, says something like; "No chance of success, sure probability of failure, certain death; what are we waiting for?" I never read the books but the movies sure had some great scenes. Maybe I should watch them again and write down the memorable lines.

Great leaders take action. They have a high standard of values they don't compromise. When action is called for and it's the right thing to do, they do it. Many leaders do what is expedient. They look for what is best for themselves. They do what makes them look good and maintain their leadership. They lead by force of personality, not character. These leaders may last a long time, but they usually rotate followers. People don't follow them for long. If they do, it's grudgingly.

Great leaders lead by strength of character. They don't manipulate, coerce or force their way. They have high values and stick to them. They are cause-oriented, purpose-driven and not self-promoting.

139

Craig S. Wagganer

NOTES

'Volving' Leadership

I saw a movie advertised called, 'Volver'. I have no idea what it's about. It got me thinking about the word. When I typed it in the last sentence it was immediately underlined with a red squiggly line meaning it isn't really a word, or at least a word recognized by my spell checker. But I came to this conclusion: great leaders are 'Volvers'. (There's that squiggly line again.)

Great leaders involve others. Leadership is not done solo or in a vacuum. Great leaders include others and make them feel worthwhile, whatever the effort (project) might be. They get involved and they motivate involvement.

Great leaders resolve conflicts. Progress at any cost is not really progress. Resolvers carefully manage and overcome conflict. Relationships are more important than accomplishments.

Great leaders evolve. Leadership usually doesn't just begin, people grow into it. Great leaders are growing leaders. That doesn't mean that they are growing just their acquisitions or accomplishments, they are growing in their leadership abilities. Great

141

leaders are always evolving into better leaders.

Great leaders have a tremendous ability to dissolve. That doesn't mean they erode into nothing, but that they are always free in sharing the credit. They never take the limelight without sharing it with others.

Great leaders are 'volvers'; involve, resolve, evolve and dissolve.

NOTES

Puzzling Lessons

I came across a picture that reminded me of an incident from several years ago…

My wife was on the floor playing with our grandson who was just a little over three years old. They were working on a 15 piece puzzle. He was having a little trouble getting the pieces together. He'd try each piece to see if it fit. He would try it one way and toss it aside if it didn't work. He'd just try it once and then try another piece. He didn't pay attention to the big picture.

My wife patiently worked with him, helping him to understand the shapes and the picture as he tried to figure out the puzzle. She arranged the pieces so they were faced the right direction. She set them so that he could make the connection between the picture on the box and the picture taking shape on the floor.

I'm not sure he actually 'got it.' He didn't finish the puzzle with much pride and joy. But immediately he was ready to dismantle it and do it again. My wife happily facilitated.

The second time as they took the pieces apart they scrambled them up; she helped him turn them the right way and orient them according to the picture. He made real progress. He looked at the picture and put each part where the picture showed. Then he'd come across pieces that went together until 'viola' the picture was completed. Two times was enough and he was quickly off to another project and play time.

I wondered if the next time he approached a puzzle if he would remember the subtle lessons his Gram taught him.

I also thought about what a great leader Gram was being. She could have easily finished the puzzle, even given him the right pieces so he could have done it 'himself', but much more quickly. Instead, she took the time to help him understand puzzles and the process. She not only helped him with that puzzle, but with other puzzles in the future.

Great leaders don't just solve puzzles, they help others understand them. They encourage others to improve their abilities, to understand processes and put pieces together.

NOTES

I Really Appreciate You Reading This...

Great leaders show appreciation, extravagantly!

In the late 1990's my mom, in her 70s, joined the computer age. She'd heard about email and thought it would be great to get a computer and learn to communicate electronically. She took a class offered at the local high school and solicited the help of a neighbor. After several lessons she was online, with an email address.

This was a great conquest for her and she was certainly excited; and rightly so. One day I received an email from her saying she'd finally got an email account and was ready to go. I thought I'd help get her started. I quickly sent out a mass email to everyone in my address book who knew my mom. I informed them that mom could now receive email and would love to hear from them.

I envisioned her getting some emails and being so excited to hear from these friends. I knew she'd love the correspondence.

145

A couple of days later I received a phone call from my daughter who was away at college. She told me she had received a thank you note from grandma in the mail. In the note, my mom thanked my daughter for emailing her. My daughter thought it was a little odd to get a thank you note for an email. When I got home from my office, I checked the mail. I had received a thank you from mom. I called my mom and asked about the note.

She informed me of her dilemma. Mom had received a ton of email, but hadn't learned how to reply. In talking with her I found out that for every email she had received she had responded with a hand written note. I thought I was helping my mother, but my efforts resulted in her spending over a hundred dollars in note cards and postage. That's how important saying "thank you" was to my mother.

I've learned a lot of things from my mother. But her demonstration of appreciation is something I'll never forget. Mom taught me to say thank you. And not just to say thank you, but to be free and extravagant in showing appreciation and recognizing the efforts of others.

NOTES

Model (Car) Leadership

When I was a kid I built a lot of model airplanes and model cars. With the help of a friend and an older sibling, I won some model car contests during my 4th and 5th grade years. We'd buy the cheapest models we could find. Then we'd build them, collect them and then make elaborate battle scenes behind our garage. We would cover everything in glue and then burn it into a trail of molten lava (plastic). Even though we didn't really know what napalm was, we would refer to it and set fire to anything that would melt or burn. We sacrificed many models and many toy soldiers that way.

For the grade school model contests, I'd buy much nicer car models. I'd get out the parts, separate them, unfold the instructions and go to work. It wouldn't be long before I'd go crying to my older brother for help. No matter how hard I tried, it never looked like the picture on the box. My brother, who was much more artistic and attentive to detail, would help me see my errors and correct them. Before long the car would take its proper form and we'd be satisfied. The car would sometimes look even better than the box because of some details my brother would include.

147

Once he helped me find a small piece of plywood and some doll rods. We painted the plywood, then covered it with pulled apart cotton balls. We took the doll rods, fashioned corner posts then connected them with some fancy yarn from my mother's sewing supplies. After this display case was completed we set the crafted model, a copper colored 1957 Chevy, carefully in the center of the cotton. Tah Dah! Not only was it a great model, but it had a nice display. I won first place. I would have been severely disappointed with anything else.

Vision is a guiding understanding of what can be and will be accomplished. Much like the picture on the model car box, it sets the ideal. But there is danger here. Too often we get too caught up in the picture. But, the key to remember is that the vision is a work in progress. It shouldn't be a final picture. It's a guiding light pulling us forward and the closer we get, the easier it is to see changes.

Don't get stuck on the original vision. Rather adapt it and improve. Don't settle for the original; always be looking to do more, accomplish more and refine more. Vision is dynamic. Great visionary leaders re-evaluate, redefine and grow the vision.

NOTES

Memory Plus

Memorial Day seems to have lots of roots. I've heard many traditions about how it got started. Even Facebook has seemingly endless reminders of how important it is to hold onto memories and honor the deceased.

My mom, as long as she was able, would use this day to visit the cemeteries that carried the markers as reminders of people she had lost. She visited and took flowers to her parents, her parents-in-law; two of her children; and would also spend time recognizing others buried alongside. Remembering roots, people and experiences were an important ingredient for thoughtfully moving forward. She modeled encouragement and inspiration by demonstrating the importance of the past influencing the future.

I had a supervisor who had a great memory and he used it well in his working relationships. He would often pass by me, or another of his reports, and make a comment like, "I was just thinking about the time you... that was a great thing you did." He was great at encouraging us by remembering our past successes and reminding of us our contributions. He modeled encouragement and inspiration by demonstrating the importance of the positives of the past influencing the future.

Great leaders remember the positives.

NOTES

Fast Food Leadership

There are several fast food places near our home. Two we prefer; one we like the sandwiches and the other we like the salads. Last week Shirley and I were on our way to a Cardinal ball game and wanted to grab a quick bite.

Which restaurant?

Both of us were leaning toward salads. As we talked about our choices something became clear. We had not talked about it previously, but the service at the restaurants were very different. The first was happy and the crew seemed to work together; they seemed to be having fun, which they included the patrons in on. The second seemed cold and distant. The employees didn't seem interested and, at times, didn't even speak loudly enough to understand.

The first seemed cleaner, with all the extra items like condiments, napkins, cup lids, and etc. all well stocked. The other, it seemed, we always had to report things being empty.

Although we were leaning toward salads, we went with sandwiches because of the preference for the better service. In our

151

discussion we also realized something that had been happening of which we had been unaware. Over the past several months when we had to choose between these two fast food places our choices were dramatic... If we were taking it home we got salads. If we were eating at the restaurant we got sandwiches.

Although we hadn't realized it, the service really did make a huge difference in our choices.

Leadership makes the difference. I would imagine the first place has leadership that is hands-on and involved making sure their people know how to relate and treat their customers. They know their jobs, and that part of the job is being customer-centered. I'll also bet that the people working there enjoy their jobs and don't see themselves as low level employees, but as part of a team that makes a difference.

My guess would be that the second restaurant is led by a person who doesn't enjoy their job and isn't able to teach other how to find enjoyment. It appears that the employees are working with an eye to when they'll get off and have little customer service training. The employees see themselves as the hired hands doing the dirty work. There is little camaraderie and little evidence of team work.

Great leaders train their people in the necessary skills of the job; which includes relationship skills. Great leaders also equip them with skills in team work and team building. Great leaders enjoy and lead others to enjoy.

NOTES

Craig S. Wagganer

Personal Best Leadership

Browsing movies at my local library I found a title, "Personal Best". I read the description and although I chose not to check it out, the title stayed with me. Leadership is all about doing your personal best. That doesn't mean doing what I can, or trying my hardest. It means a commitment to the ideal of achieving the highest, most honorable, best case scenario for everyone. Personal best leadership causes everyone to rise above their personal best to a synergy that redefines 'best'. It exceeds all expectations.

I came across an anonymous quote a few years ago that impressed me.

"Excellence can be achieved if you...

Risk more than others think is safe,

Love more than others think is wise,

Dream more than others think is practical,

And expect more than others think is possible."

Great leadership is excellence in character continually setting new personal records.

155

Craig S. Wagganer

NOTES

Pitching Leadership

I was watching the celebration of the St. Louis Cardinals after they had defeated the Milwaukee Brewers for the National League Pennant. Being a Cardinals fan, I was enjoying watching joy being displayed. In the interviews with the players and coaches, each one gave credit to others. Any time one person was given an accolade they would pass it on and give credit to other teammates and to the organization. Player after player gave credit to other players, coaches and administrators. Coaches gave credit to players and administrators. Administrators gave credit to the players and coaches. It was clear everyone recognized the victory as an organizational accomplishment.

When Tony Larussa was heralded for a great team and great decisions; he immediately turned to his pitching coach; Dave Duncan, (who was not present because of his wife's illness). As much praise as was given to Mr. Larussa, he was passing it all on to the man he believed was greatly responsible.

Great leaders give credit where credit is due and even more so. If a person truly wants to be a great leader they will learn to make the most of every opportunity. It's vitally important to recognize the greatness in

157

others and to draw attention to it as much as possible. Great leaders make heroes of others.

NOTES

Leader Up!

During the 2011 National League Baseball Divisional Playoffs, the St. Louis Cardinals were playing the Milwaukee Brewers. It was possibly the last home game for Prince Fielder in a Brewers uniform.

Recognizing that, and his tremendous contributions over his time there, he was given a rousing ovation by the fans. It wasn't quite over when the pitcher stood on the mound for the next pitch. Albert Pujols, recognizing the situation, called time so that the fans could continue showing their appreciation for their hero. By calling time, Albert allowed the acclamation to continue and even grow. Mr. Fielder recognized what Mr. Pujols had done and acknowledged it. So did the fans–they were grateful.

There is some irony here. Albert is in the exact same position as Prince. Both may be ending illustrious careers with their professional teams. Each player has only played for one team during their careers. Now, both may be moving on to larger markets.

Albert's display was a great show of sportsmanship and leadership. He's recognized as a leader on and off the field.

Albert showed a tremendous level of leadership by calling time. Great leadership is concerned with equity. Albert recognized the greatness of Prince. He helped Prince to drink in the fan admiration. Albert would have been fine if no one recognized him. He didn't do it for himself. He had the foresight and quick response to take charge and make it right. Great leaders aren't as concerned with being recognized as they are with recognizing true greatness.

NOTES

Little Behaviors,

Big Lessons

How does leadership show itself in small things?

It's a funny feeling when you go up to a door that obviously says "Push" on it and it doesn't open. You step back and read it again and then check to see if you can find a lock. Someone behind then says, "Pull." You do, and the door opens. In that quick second when you pull the door open you notice the word "Push" was printed backwards – it was for people on the other side of the door. On your side the word "Pull" was clearly displayed on the handle.

It's kind of like what happens when you approach an automatic door and almost walk into the stationary glass because the sliding part went from right to left and you approached the door as if it were left to right.

Spending quite a bit of time in airports, I often find myself at a sink with my hands under the faucet waiting for the water to start. I move my hands back and forth and nothing. Finally, I realize it's a regular faucet with handles, not the type with the sensors.

161

It's the funny sensation of taking things for granted; the mind is quickly processing info although it doesn't process that the word is backwards, or recognize the handles on faucets, or which way a door will slide open.

Also funny is our reaction... Why would they put the message on one side of the door on the glass and the other on the handle? It's their mistake not mine – I'm an innocent victim.

Why wasn't the door marked with an arrow showing which way it was to slide – their mistake, not mine. Faucet handles should be clearly marked "hot" and "cold" then I would have noticed – their mistake, not mine. If the sign, "Pull Down, Tear Up" were bigger then I wouldn't be waiving my hands in front of the paper towel dispenser waiting for them to automatically respond - their mistake, not mine...

These little things reveal leadership. Great leaders have the ability to laugh at themselves, admit their foibles and enjoy being vulnerable with their team.

NOTES

One Cent Lesson

How much is a penny worth?

Good question. The accompanying question got me thinking, "Is it worth a bend over?"

The implication is astounding in very simple form. Is a penny worth the effort it takes to bend over and pick it up? Some would say yes, others no. Each is right according to the value they place on the penny.

The value of the coin is determined by what the individual is willing to give for it. A young person may quickly bend over without hesitation. A person with back or leg problems may walk past without thought.

The value of anything is not necessarily inherent in the object, but rather is determined by the perspective of those evaluating.

This is an important lesson for leaders. The value of your leadership is not based on your perception of yourself and your contribution; but rather the value of your leadership is determined by those you lead.

It is good to ask questions and learn from the answers.

163

NOTES

What Was the Elephant's Perspective?

I love the poem, "The Blind Men and the Elephant" by John Godfrey Saxe (1816-1887). It is a good lesson for leaders. Great leaders understand their own limitations and don't jump to conclusions, or rule out someone else because of differences.

Perception is reality, but great leaders know there is much more to reality than their own perception.

Enjoy.

"It was six men of Indostan

To learning much inclined,

Who went to see the Elephant

(Though all of them were blind),

That each by observation

Might satisfy his mind.

The First approached the Elephant,

And happening to fall

Against his broad and sturdy side,

At once began to bawl:

"God bless me! but the Elephant

Is very like a WALL!"

The Second, feeling of the tusk,

Cried, "Ho, what have we here,

So very round and smooth and sharp?

To me 'tis mighty clear

This wonder of an Elephant

Is very like a SPEAR!"

The Third approached the animal,

And happening to take

The squirming trunk within his hands,

Thus boldly up and spake:

"I see," quoth he, "the Elephant

Is very like a SNAKE!"

The Fourth reached out an eager hand,

And felt about the knee

"What most this wondrous beast is like

Is mighty plain," quoth he:

"'Tis clear enough the Elephant

Is very like a TREE!"

The Fifth, who chanced to touch the ear,

Said: "E'en the blindest man

Can tell what this resembles most;

Deny the fact who can,

This marvel of an Elephant

Is very like a FAN!"

The Sixth no sooner had begun

About the beast to grope,

Than seizing on the swinging tail

That fell within his scope,

"I see," quoth he, "the Elephant

Is very like a ROPE!"

167

And so these men of Indostan

Disputed loud and long,

Each in his own opinion

Exceeding stiff and strong,

Though each was partly in the right,

And all were in the wrong!"

NOTES

Eyeing Perspectives

There's a little fish that has an amazing ability. The Anablep's eyes are made in such a fashion that it can see above and below the water's surface at the same time. The pupil in each eye is horizontally divided into two parts, allowing it to see and focus on two perspectives. It hangs out at the water's surface and can see above and below the water simultaneously searching for food and watching for danger.

Leaders can learn a valuable lesson from these little South American fish. We need to see from multiple perspectives. Too often we are only interested in our own opinion. We may give lip service to others, but not serious consideration. After all, we are the leader, it is our job to lead, and others are to follow. But what a fallacy.

Great leaders listen and seek to understand the voice and reasoning of others. They try to understand perspectives so they can make good decisions that benefit the entire team. They value dissent that is authentic and of integrity. They are not afraid or threatened by others. They have a security as well as a vulnerability because what they do and accomplish is based on teamwork, not personal ego.

Seeing and understanding from differing perspectives is a skill for leaders to focus on, practice and demonstrate for future leaders. Great leaders see from and look for multiple perspectives.

NOTES

3 Keys to Effective

Communication

I was recently asked about leadership communication. After quite a discussion, I decided there are three primary considerations for a leader when communicating with others; whether publicly or privately. First, the leader takes responsibility for communication. Which means the leader makes sure communication happens. There is no room for assumption. The leader must make sure s/he understands - and is understood. If the message is flawed or unclear and misunderstanding happens, the leader takes responsibility for the miscommunication.

Secondly, the leader is honest in all communication. This isn't easy, but it is expedient. The leader must be open and transparent in all communication. It's better to get problems out in the open than to have them surface later. No one wants to field questions about why the truth wasn't told from the beginning. If after telling the truth you have to explain it, then your intention was to mislead. I learned at an early age to just be completely honest and tell the truth. Never tell only part of the truth for 'safety sake'. Never tell the truth with the intention of using it to mislead. Tell the whole truth.

Third, always be encouraging. Use words to encourage and uplift others. Give others a sense of empowerment and confidence in their abilities. Use constructive communication, especially if the truth is threatening or damaging. Learn to communicate in a way that not only encourages the recipient, but gives them a model to look up to and emulate.

Being an effective communicator means: taking responsibility for the communication, being honest about what you communicate and encouraging your listeners.

NOTES

A Perfect Union

It's an age old problem. I talked with a man who was given responsibility for a project, but had no authority to actualize the plan. He was told to follow directions and complete the project. He had questions and needed to make decisions, but he wasn't given the authority to complete the project. With every step or question, he had to go back to the person in authority. The "authority person" was frustrated with the interruptions. The "responsible party" was frustrated with the paralysis.

Leaders must realize: leading means having authority and responsibility. When taking on a leadership situation it must be understood that authority comes with the responsibility. Neither one can work effectively without the other. To give a person authority without responsibility is tyranny. To give responsibility without authority is manipulation.

Authority and responsibility is the marriage that unites and creates effective leadership within an individual. Understanding this "marriage" enables today's leaders to train the next generation of leaders.

NOTES

A Question Worthy

of Action.

I love small jets and small airports, but they have their disadvantages. Flying home from Ohio, I was booked to fly out of the Toledo airport. A small airport served by only one airline. They have three flights in/out a day, all to/from O'Hare airport in Chicago. So when I arrived at the Toledo airport for my early afternoon flight and found that O'Hare was currently shut down; I knew all the flights from Toledo had been cancelled.

My choices were to wait until the next open spot on a flight out of Toledo, which was about 8:00 PM the next night. Or, I could drive to Detroit to catch a plane to Minneapolis, and then on home to St. Louis.

I rented a car and headed for Detroit, only an hour's drive away. When I arrived at the Detroit airport, the inconveniences of the O'Hare shut down were apparent. Traveler stress levels were high. And the stress of the ticketing agents was also high. Even the stress levels at security had been equally pushed to the limit - for travelers and workers alike. At the gate, nothing had changed. The stress was visibly recognizable. It was very easy to see what

175

travelers were being interrupted by the O'Hare ordeal and which airline staff were handling those stressed travelers.

A man sat down next to me and said, "Well, what can you do?" That made me think.

I got up and stood in one of the lines handling the stressed out travelers. I waited my turn in line and finally got to the ticket counter. I'm sure I seemed rude, but I asked the attendant to wait until I got the other service person's attention. I then explained to them, "I know you're having a rough day. You're handling problems for unhappy people and you're doing the best you can in a very difficult situation. It's not your fault – or theirs. Could I bring you a cup of coffee, water or cold drink? And I'd be delighted if you would let me bring you a snack. What would you like?"

That counter got very quiet. The workers declined my offer, but almost gushed with appreciation for the show of support. The people behind me in line became noticeably more patient. I hadn't anticipated that this little gesture would be a stress reliever for all those who noticed. I went and purchased a couple waters. I returned to the counter, explaining it was the least I could do to show my appreciation for their hard work. They were taking the brunt of people's frustration while trying to satisfy every traveler's demands.

Maybe when faced with problem situations a good question to ask is, "What can I do?" And then do something . . . positive.

NOTES

Craig S. Wagganer

A Winning Losing Season

A group of people brought breakfast to support a local high school football team. The players were all very appreciative and so were the coaches. It was also great to see the interaction and observe the relationships between the players, the coaches and the community members who had come bringing food.

Several times throughout the brief encounter, announcements had to be made. It's not easy to get the attention of over 30 high school football players. But one thing was clear. When the coach spoke, they listened.

It was easy to see that the attention given the coach was not the result of fear or consequences. The coach was well-liked and respected. The head coach, as well as the rest of the coaching staff, cared greatly about the kids.

In talking with the coaches I learned that their concern went way beyond the football field. I heard their stories of personal sacrifice of time, energy and money. The coach and his staff had supported the players not just for their contributions to the football team, but also in their personal lives. It was

179

a joy to talk with the team members and coaches, but a greater honor to observe the situation.

They were not a great football team. Their record for the season was a losing one. The day we served breakfast turned out to be their last game of the season - a losing effort in the first playoff game.

But the leadership displayed by the coach and his staff exhibited how much they cared. Great leadership cares. Great leadership understands that the most important things may not be revealed in the score. Maybe the most important thing a coach can demonstrate isn't won on the field, but is the caring shown off the field.

NOTES

Articulate to the Audience

I was at a meeting of leaders last week and overheard an interesting conversation. Two men were talking about their leadership roles and responsibilities. As one talked it was clear he chose his words carefully and had given thought as to how to introduce himself. The other spoke well, but used a lot of slang trying to make his point. It was interesting.

Both men dressed like business leaders. They continued their conversation after introductions were made. They both spoke clearly. There was one difference. The first leader used very descriptive and articulate language. The other leader was very casual and used phrases I found interesting. Phrases like, "You know what I mean?" "You see where I'm coming from…" "You follow?" and "You know what I'm talking about."

As I write this I'm using correct spelling, not the spelling that may be a better representative of what I'm writing. "You understand?"

Am I saying one is a better leader than the other, or one spoke more correctly than the other? Not necessarily. But I will say this.

181

Good leaders are articulate and explain themselves using concise understandable terminology. They don't rely on slang or inappropriate language. Let's face it, clarity creates better understanding and therefore greater communication. The bigger issue here is if great leaders know and understand their audience.

NOTES

Hearing Enough to Ask

It was an interesting situation. I had given directions for a team building activity. The directions are purposely pretty vague. It's up to the groups to figure out how to accomplish the task. Throughout my brief description, certain covert clues are given so that, if listening, the groups will be helped in knowing what to do. In fact, it's pretty simple - if you're listening.

After the directions were given. One group, under the direction of one individual, began to work out the problem. There were a lot of questions and the leader quickly took charge trying to answer every one with his own thoughts. There was a lot of confusion and some frustration; as the leader started making everyone conform to his ideas. I watched them closely until I was interrupted.

A leader from another group had quieted his group's clamor of questions and asked them to wait for a minute. He then approached me for clarification. I made the clarification and they completed the challenge quickly. This leader was listening. He knew the key to solving the problem was simply to ask me for the information I had previously left out.

183

The first group continued with their frustration building. Several members just gave up and became observers. There was quite a contentious scene brewing. I was about to step in when one of the group's members noticed the other group was finished, and enjoying the fruits of their labor. It was brought to the leader's attention. A little embarrassed, he approached the other team and asked how they figured it out so quickly. The second group responded, almost as one, "We asked him," pointing at me.

Great leaders listen intently and ask questions.

NOTES

Hold the Pain

The doctor said the original problem was bone spurs. The pain caused by the spurs caused me to limit my movement. The limited movement caused scar tissue to form which increased the pain which further limited movement. This eventually led to surgery to remove the bone spurs and scar tissue.

So part of the problem is pain. Old Doc Campbell (from television's Hee Haw fame), was approached by a patient who was making a motion with his arm saying, "It hurts when I do this." Doc responded, "Well, don't do that!"

My first response to pain is to stop whatever I'm doing that is causing the pain. But now, after shoulder surgery, I'm in physical therapy. I've been given five exercises to do three times a day. They are to stretch the muscles and to keep the scar tissue from reforming. Basically the instructions are to stretch the muscle until it hurts, then hold that to a count of ten, then relax for a ten count. And then to repeat nine more times.

My reaction to pain has always been to stop. But they reassure me that the pain I'm experiencing now will prevent pain and mobility problems in the future. It is the scare of future problems that causes me to endure the pain of therapy.

Great leaders understand that stretching is painful. Great leaders effectively communicate that future victories are worth the present suffering. Sometimes it is necessary to endure short term pain for a long term solution. This doesn't mean that all pain is good, or that leaders can inflict painful situations at will. But there are times when providing for growth through long-term vision, means painful stretching today. Great leaders communicate the value of the process - and the pain.

NOTES

Inutshuk Leadership

While traveling on Victoria Island, my wife and I came across an 'inutshuk'; a pile of stones stacked to resemble a human body. Two legs, a body, arms and a head are clearly visible. The stones are stacked in such a way that you know it was no accident. There's a lot more to the history, but our first questions were answered by a person who told us this stone stacking was an Inuit Indian practice used to notify other groups of safe passage.

When other bands of Native Americans, or anyone who understood the sign, came across an 'inutshuk' they would readily know this was a safe area. It was safe to pass this way. We were also told that different variations of the rock formation could have different meanings; such as good fishing, a memorial, or an abode of the spirits. Whatever the meaning, an 'inutshuk' was placed to give some sort of notice to others.

On every picture or portrayal of these fantastic structures there was never a signature. The person(s) making the large stone monuments didn't take credit for what they had done.

Craig S. Wagganer

Great leaders place 'inutshuks'. With their team they often blaze a trail, make new discoveries, lead the way and are innovative. They let others know of safe passage and pave the way for others to follow.

NOTES

188

Leadership Tea

Interesting movie, "Tea with Mussolini". Two of the characters are an interesting study. Elsa is a rich Jewish–American socialite with an entertainment background. She's outgoing and flamboyant. Lady Hester is the widow of an English Ambassador and an acquaintance of Mussolini. She's very proper and reserved.

Elsa is carefree and generous, while Lady Hester is concerned with appearances and being dignified. Elsa is forgiving, Lady Hester is brooding. Both women exude influence upon those around them. They are very much in leadership positions; not by rank or position, but by influence. Elsa is concerned about helping and doing what is right. But Lady Hester is bitter and manipulative with her gossip. Lady Hester believes there isn't any question of right or wrong, other than what is proper and "English".

Throughout the movie, Elsa's ability to influence increases as Lady Hester loses hers. Great leaders lead by their drive, strong character and compassion, not by manipulation or coercion.

189

NOTES

Memorial Stones

Going through some old photos I found some from a trip to Israel. One of the more fascinating things our guide and team leader taught us was practice of memorial stones. The ritual dates back to Biblical times. Passing through the Judean wilderness, (which is more like a rocky desert), we would occasionally come across a few stones stacked upon each other.

Our guide asked us if we knew how the stones got there. Of course we looked at each other, the answer being too obvious to actually make a comment. "Whenever you see stones stacked upon each other that means someone has been there to do it," he stated. We smiled at the obvious as he went on to tell why a person would stack the stones.

People in that area will stack stones as a memorial. When you see a stack of stones it means something significant in the life of the person happened there. The stones are a reminder of the incident to the person who stacked them, and maybe to their family or travel companions. No one unrelated to the story behind the stones may know the reason they are stacked at that place. But the intended audience will know being

191

reminded of the significant event whenever they pass that way.

This tradition is time-honored, so no one will destroy the markers out of respect for the memory and experience represented. When others pass by, they may be reminded of their own memorial stone stories. This tradition is well-respected and valued among the people of that area.

Great leaders celebrate successes with their team. They create "memorial stones".

NOTES

Nice Example

Writer Dave Barry has said, "A person who is nice to you, but rude to the waiter, is not a nice person."

This past week I had the experience of working with two bosses from different companies. One boss was a sincerely nice person. During all of our conversations, she was a kind, considerate and careful listener. I noticed when others were talking with her, she was the same way. She was a nice person with me, her staff, the hotel staff and everyone I saw her interact with.

The other person I worked with was very nice to me, exhibiting the same qualities as mentioned above concerning the previous boss. However, I noticed a difference in this person when he dealt with others "under" his authority. He was belligerent, intimidating, and demanding to them. It made me uncomfortable to work with him, even to be around him. I felt sorry for those who worked for him; because he was so abrupt and rude.

I believe this to be true. Leaders don't have to be nice. But, great leaders, effective leaders, are nice people.

NOTES

Presenting Your Presence

There were several people gathered. A disagreement arose as people were trying to choose the best course of action. There were predominantly two leaders with different voices describing the situation. One voice was loud, demanding; intimidating. The other calm and reserved. The first voice was animated and spontaneous. The second, quietly articulated a plan of action. The two voices were very different in their point of view, and in how they communicated what they believed to be right.

As the minutes that passed, it seeming like hours. It was clear the first voice was growing louder and dissatisfied. There was frustration in the second voice, but it remained focused. The first voice became divided but strongly held to its point of view and kept struggling to insure it would win.

The two leaders had taken very different actions. The first leader was loud and intimidating, insisting on their way. The second, calm and logical, trying to understand and offer resolutions. At times, the debate became so heated it seemed no solution would be reached; some swayed by the loud voice, afraid to disagree. Others convinced by the logic and calm of the second.

The resolution? Put yourself in this situation, who would you have followed? Which leader would you have been?

Great leaders have a strong presence but not necessarily the loudest voice.

NOTES

Relative Importance

Yesterday I spent a little time with my dad. When I arrived, he was eating breakfast. He's been more alert and energetic during the past week. It's good to see him in better spirits and more active physically. In December, he'll be 91 and he's doing great - considering.

We sat and talked for a few moments. I asked if he would like to go for a ride; maybe drive through Lone Elk Park? The park has elk, deer, buffalo and other critters. "Yes, it sounds like fun," he said, to my surprise. Usually when given an opportunity to get out of the house, he complains about a knee hurting, being too tired, or gives some other excuse to stay at home in his recliner.

Yesterday he said yes. He got dressed and put on a light jacket. It was a nice drive. We saw quite a few elk. They were all laying down, so we didn't get too good a look at them. They appeared more like rocks than animals.

The buffalo were so far away, you really couldn't tell what they were. If we hadn't been in the park, we probably wouldn't have recognized them. We spotted several deer,

197

a couple close enough to count the points on their antlers and a couple of does. It was nice to see the wildlife but even better to get Dad out. Dad grew up in the country and has always loved being in the woods. Recently, that hasn't been a reality for him. The best part was watching him out of the corner of my eye as he looked around, drinking it all in.

I'm glad I wasn't so busy yesterday and that Dad and I had time together. Everyone talks about how relationships are most important, but then we let other things take our precious time.

Gotta go, I have some important phone calls and appointments to make. Maybe you do, too.

NOTES

Self Leadership

Leadership begins with character.

A lot is said about a leader's influence and each person's sphere of influence. It's true that everyone is a leader to some degree, whether they realize or admit it, or not. Everyone wields some influence. That influence begins with self.

Self-leadership is where character is formed. It's the values you hold and the fervency with which you hold them, that determines your ability to lead. A person's integrity and how they lead themselves, will determine the extent and effectiveness of their leadership of others.

We must first conquer our own leadership dilemmas before we can confidently allow others to follow us. That simply means we must be self-aware and self-disciplined.

Self-awareness is knowing who you are. It is understanding your strengths and weaknesses; talents, gifts and abilities, as well as your shortcomings, prejudices, and frailties. It's knowing what you are good at and what you can and cannot do. It is to knowing when you can trust yourself and when you need to ask for help.

Self-discipline helps us maintain integrity and be self-motivated and self-controlled. Self-discipline is the ability to do what needs to be done when it needs to be done.

The first order of leadership is mastering your self.

NOTES

Stepping Out

It was a great display and lesson in leadership. There was a community need. Many people were thinking about what they might do, how they could contribute to help and be supportive to people in the community. But one woman took action.

She developed a plan. Then she set it in motion. As she worked her plan, others came along to help and they promoted her brilliant idea. In the end, one woman took the lead and several people got involved. In the end, a community received aid.

Great leaders step out. They take initiative, recruit help and provide opportunities. This great leader did it for a great cause.

NOTES

Craig S. Wagganer

Thank You, Second Fiddlers

This is the 50th anniversary of the March on Washington that included Dr. M. L. King's famous speech remembered as 'I Have a Dream.' I've been reading a little about the occasion and about the people involved. I have also been reading about the civil rights movement; its progress and the work still needing to be done.

I remember reading a quote, reportedly from Leonard Bernstein, that the hardest instrument to play is second fiddle. As I read and watched some internet recordings, I was impressed by all the people that history doesn't record who were instrumental in making a difference. Often times it's the leader who motivates and gets recognized. Little is known about the anonymous individuals who've sacrificed and made the commitments that also facilitate change.

Soloists are fantastic and much appreciated, but it is the blending of sounds that makes the orchestra.

Leaders step up to champion forward, but for leaders to be effective, there must be followers. Followers who accept their responsibility for the cause. When someone

203

learns to play second fiddle effectively they've found an important role.

Here's to those who exhibit personal leadership that supports a cause and truly makes the difference. If it weren't for the countless numbers who have learned to play second fiddle (follow) effectively, there would be no great leaders. And no great victories. Thank you to the countless thousands who have made a positive difference without making the headlines.

NOTES

The Action Now Ability

I heard a man talking. He stated that he's a man who gets things done. He admitted he has little compassion and is not a counselor. But when something needs be addressed or get done, he can make it happen. He is not reticent when approaching a person who needs to be confronted on an issue. He is confident in his ability to evaluate situations and work out reasonable and agreeable solutions. He gets irritated if he has trouble overcoming or is unsure how to address a problem. His biggest frustration is when a situation looms in front of him without resolution. But he will always take action.

As I observed this person over a period of time, I found that he is right in his self-evaluation. He is extremely confident in his talents and abilities. This is a very important quality in leadership. Great leaders are good evaluators and are also good at taking action. All leaders may not feel confident in their ability to address problems, or problem people. But it's a skill leaders develop and then use when necessary. Great leaders know how to confront situations and people. Knowing how to resolve a problem quickly can often save time, effort, money and ward off more significant problems in the future. Readily addressing a problem when it

205

occurs can keep it from escalating into a larger, more insurmountable problem.

Great leaders may not always feel confident in what they have to do, but they know the importance of taking action to do what is necessary. Even if it is out of their comfort zone.

NOTES

The Leader's Perspective

I saw an interesting video that offered a neat challenge. The instructions were simple but the results a little surprising. All you need to do is put your arms up and out to the sides of your body, with your elbows bent at 90 degrees. Palms open and facing forward. Keep your eyes looking forward, (you'll only see your hands if you have great peripheral vision). First, touch your right index finger to your nose and then return your hand to the previous position. Then, touch your right index finger and the tip of your thumb on your left hand, and then return to the resting position. Touch your nose again and return to the resting position. Now, with your right hand, touch the tip of your index finger on the left hand. Continue this, alternating touching your nose with your right index finger and each finger on your left hand, until you have touched each finger on your left hand with the index finger on your right.

Now try the same exercise with your eyes closed.

Why is it with your eyes open you are able to touch each finger, but with your eyes closed you come close, but miss the tips or the entire hand? It's a funny feeling.

Apparently with your eyes open, even though you can't see your hands you're still able to keep your spatial awareness. So even though your hands are out of sight, the awareness of where your hands are is clearer because you can identify where you are in your surroundings.

With your eyes closed, your spatial awareness is limited. The task becomes more challenging; almost impossible.

Great leaders lead with their eyes open.

NOTES

The Leaders Voice

I have family members who watch the TV reality show, 'The Voice'. I haven't seen it. Listening to my wife and daughter talk about it, I found a statement made by one of the cast members worthwhile.

I am not sure the situation but apparently one of the singers who was competing had sung several times and gotten better each time. The panel that evaluates the singers was very encouraging of the young star. One of those panel members stated that their show is about encouraging talent and that is why they have coaches, not judges.

Leadership is more about coaching than judging. Isaiah 30:21 says, "And your ear shall hear a word behind you saying, "this is the way, walk in it.'" That's leadership. It's more about a voice from behind; guiding, than it's about a voice in front; telling.

Jesus' leadership model was much more coaching than judging. He empowered his followers to become leaders who coached others in the way they should go. Jesus was so effective in leading his followers that he created a legacy of generational believers. His ability to empower his followers can be traced down to the present number of faithful Christians.

Jesus' model of leadership was the voice behind saying "This is the way, walk in it." He was not about power, but about empowering others to be his people. Jesus empowered his followers to be all they could be.

Maybe a good description of leadership is coaching. It's not about power, it is about empowering.

NOTES

Therapeutic Information

Today was my last day of physical therapy after my shoulder surgery two months ago.

The two months of visiting the therapist a couple times a week, along with daily exercises, has brought progress , but not without pain. The exercises and the stretching has been excruciating at times. But I know the importance of getting the joint and muscles back in shape and stretched to normal limitations. The surgery was necessary to repair and remove problems that had developed. Therapy was necessary to restore previous loss and prevent further complications.

I've learned a lot of lessons through the experience. I could say a lot about the surgery and therapy and about leadership repairing situations, removing problems, restoring loss, and preventing complications. All great lessons with tremendous applications. But through this process the most important thing has been communication. As I went through the surgery and the therapy I knew the reasons for every step of the way. At no point was I left wondering 'why?' at any circumstance or situation. I knew what was being done and the reasons why. I was given all the

211

information and helped make the important decisions.

Great leaders keep people informed. They know that information is the most important ingredient to understanding and shared responsibility. They place a high priority on communication and the breadth and depth of information. They would rather risk giving out too much information instead of too little. Clear, accurate information is the necessary key to handling the responsibility of communication.

NOTES

The End

About the Author

Craig Wagganer is the owner and Chief Creative Officer of LeadersBridge. LeadersBridge provides the very best in team building workshops, leadership training, public speaking skills training and keynote addresses. Craig can be contacted through the company website at LeadersBridge.com.

Author's Note

Thank you for reading this little book. I hope you enjoyed and benefited from the experience. I hope you took notes, I hope you were challenged and provoked. I hope that having read it once, you'll visit it again. Most of all I hope you were influenced in a positive way.

Craig S. Wagganer

Craig S. Wagganer

49242486R00129

Made in the USA
Charleston, SC
22 November 2015